Journal of the
Albert Camus Society

2010

www.Camus-Society.com

Journal of the Albert Camus Society

The purpose of the *Journal of the Albert Camus Society* is to further understanding of the work and thought of Albert Camus.

The material contained in this journal represents the opinions of the authors and not necessarily those of the Albert Camus Society or anyone affiliated with the Society.

Authors – paper submissions

In the first instance email an abstract of no more than 300 words to secretary@camus-society.com

For more information on submissions we refer you to the guidelines printed at the end of this journal.

Copyright

ISBN 978-1-4467-9023-6

Table of Contents

Journal of Camus Studies

Coming soon...

This is the second Journal of the Albert Camus Society and the last. In 2011, the Albert Camus Societies of the UK and US will put out a new **Journal of Camus Studies**. The Editor-in-Chief of this new journal will be Peter Francev, President of the Albert Camus Society of the US.

The Journal of Camus Studies will be out in late 2011.

For submission guidelines please turn to page 129.

Simon Lea
President, Albert Camus Society of the UK

Human Nature and The Absurd in *The Stranger, Caligula* and *Cross Purpose*

By Simon Lea

In this paper I will be comparing three of Camus's characters: one from a novel and two from plays. The novel is *The Stranger* and the character is, of course, Meursault. The two plays are *Caligula* and *Cross Purpose*; the characters: *Caligula* and *Martha* respectively. While Caligula has a real-life counterpart, the character we see in Camus's play is not supposed to be an accurate representation of the man. The actual Roman Emperor may, or may not, bear close resemblance to the title character of the play, but we are only interested in the Caligula Camus created, not the historical figure. Martha is also a work of fiction and so is Patrice Meursault. In what follows, I will be claiming that Meursault is an unreal character and that the events that occur in *The Stranger* are also unreal. Obviously, the characters and events in the two plays are works of fiction and did not occur in 'real life'. My point will be that unlike Caligula and Martha, Meursault could not exist in real life. That is, he is not real enough to be an illustration of an actual person experiencing the Absurd. In fact, this being so, it would be a mistake to take Meursault as an example; certainly not one to follow. Rather misleadingly, Camus once referred to this character with 'ironic affection' as "the only Christ that we deserve."[1] The person we usually associate with the title Christ, is Jesus of Nazareth. According to Christians he possesses two paradoxical qualities: a human nature and a God nature; he was the God-Man. Meursault does not contain two natures. Camus did not intend to make him a god but he didn't make him human either. In the first half of this paper (sections I-III) I will look at the character of Meursault and the unreality of the man and the events that surround him. In the second half (sections IV-VI) I will, by comparison with Caligula and Martha, look at the role human nature plays in the Absurd.

---

1   Albert Camus, *Afterword*, The Outsider (Penguin 1982) p.118

I *an unreal crime*

In 1955 Camus commented on *The Stranger*, "A long time ago I summed up *The Stranger* in a sentence which I realize is extremely paradoxical: 'In our society any man who doesn't cry at his mother's funeral is liable to be condemned to death'. I simply meant that the hero of the book is condemned because he doesn't play the game."[2]

The way Meursault does not play the game, according to his author, is that "he refuses to lie"[3]. Being truthful is a virtue that can get you killed. If you commit a capital offense and don't lie to the police, you'll end up dead. Even if you didn't do it, telling the truth is no protection against miscarriages of justice and you may well be killed. The hero of *The Stranger* does not find himself condemned to death simply because he didn't cry at his mother's funeral and it wasn't because he refused to lie in court. It would be a sick joke for a convicted murderer to claim he's in prison, not because he killed a man, but rather because he got caught or because he didn't lie in court. Meursault was in court because he shot and killed a man.

Camus gives no reason for Meursault's crime; he commits a senseless murder. He doesn't have him shoot the Arab or even pull the trigger, rather, "[Meursault's] whole being went tense and [he] tightened [his] grip on the gun. The trigger gave [.]"[4] Compare this account of someone being shot with the following two examples:

1. I looked him in the eye, felt the gun in my hand and lifted it to his face which twisted in horror. I pulled the trigger and shot him dead.

2. The sun was shining directly in my eyes blinding me. There was a noise like someone had opened the door and was walking into the room. I stuck out my arm to stop whoever had entered from walking into me but my hand knocked against a heavy object on the shelf. A loud bang filled the room. I

---

2   Ibid

3   Ibid

4   Albert Camus, *The Outsider* (Penguin 1983) p.60

had knocked Raymond's gun to the floor and on impact it had discharged, shooting the Arab.

In (1) it looks as if the narrator intended to shoot and kill someone. In (2) the Arab is killed by accident. It would be incorrect to say that he fired the gun when all he did was knock it to the floor. Camus doesn't have Meursault kill the Arab by accident; however, he chooses to describe the shooting in terms of his hero tightening his grip on the gun's handle and the trigger giving way, rather than a simple point and shoot. The circumstances that lead up to the event are not incomprehensible; we may not understand exactly why Meursault shoots but we can see how he ended up standing in front of a man with a gun in his hand. There is a good reason why Meursault has a gun; that is he is not carrying a weapon because he intends to harm anyone. The Arab is described as threatening; not only is he someone who is already linked by violence to Meursault, he is carrying a weapon himself: "the Arab drew his knife and held it out towards me in the sun. The light leapt off the steel and it was like a long, flashing sword lunging at my forehead."[5]

Camus could have had Meursault involved with a different kind of killing. Perhaps, back at his apartment, Raymond asks him to look after his gun or even slips the gun into Meursault's pocket when he hears a policeman knock on the door. Later, while Meursault rides the tram, he feels the weapon in his pocket, a shard of sunlight pierces his eyes, and he pulls the gun from his pocket and fires it into the face of the old lady sitting opposite him. Or walking down the street, he discovers the gun in his pocket, a dog barks, and Meursault fires into a passing pram, then four more times into the mother, "like giving four sharp knocks at the door of unhappiness."[6]

The problem for Camus is that he wants his hero to commit a crime he is then innocent of. Meursault needs to be innocent of murder so he can then be condemned to death for not crying at his mother's funeral rather than for killing a man. Of course, before he can be condemned he needs to be put on trial, so he has to commit a capital offense. If the Arab hadn't been

---

5   Ibid.

6   Ibid

murdered, if Meursault had returned home after an uneventful trip, he would have presumably continued to live his life, unnoticed and not condemned by society. Society does not actually condemn men for not crying at their mother's funeral; it is doubtful Society would even notice such a man at all.

Meursault's crime is unreal; he shoots an Arab but is innocent of murder. He isn't guilty of manslaughter, going too far in attempting to defend himself. A good case could have been made for the latter, but Camus needs Meursault's crime to be forgotten by the reader. Meursault has a hard time remembering that he is a criminal himself! For the second half of the novel, Meursault must have our sympathy, and this is why, I believe, Camus did not have him shooting into the face of an old lady or into a passing pram. And why Meursault is personalized but the Arab is not. Camus doesn't want us sympathizing with the victim, so he doesn't give us a victim to sympathize with. The shooting of the Arab, Meursault's unreal crime, is solely an event necessary to get us from the first half of the novel to the second.

II *an unreal man*

Meursault is put on trial because he murdered an Arab. Taking into account that at that time in Algeria a white man accused of killing an Arab would probably escape justice, Meursault doesn't (more unreality?). At the trial, the prosecution, in order to make sense of the crime, look to the personality of the accused. What is he like? A man who doesn't honour his dead mother, who is friends with a pimp, who shoots and kills a man and then shows no kind of remorse whatsoever. One of the problems many readers of *The Stranger* have is that they can not reconcile the fact that Meursault is a murderer; he is the bad guy yet Camus obviously wants us to sympathize with him. The problem is that Meursault does not just commit an unreal crime, he is an unreal person. Even the prosecutor at the trial appears to notice there is something unbelievable about Meursault:

> "Raymond said that it was quite *by chance* that I happened to be on the beach. The prosecutor then asked how it was that the letter which lay behind the intrigue had been written by me. Raymond replied that it was *by chance*. The prosecutor retorted that *chance* already had a number of misdemeanors on its conscience in this affair. He wanted to know if it was *by chance* that I hadn't

intervened when Raymond had beaten up his mistress, *by chance* that I had acted as a witness at the police station, and also *by chance* that the statements I'd made on that occasion had proved to be so thoroughly accommodating." (My emphasis added)[7]

The prosecutor is right, there does seem to be too much riding on chance in this story. With so many chance events, all working together to get Meursault where he is, one 'suspects' an intelligent designer, an author, behind it all. Could this be a case of Camus's philosophy spilling over into his character and sticking out like a sore thumb?[8] If Meursault's crime seems unreal, as well as the events that lead up to it, and to his being in court – this is because Meursault himself is unreal. Meursault is *literally* an invented character, created to tell a story, but what story? Is *The Stranger* a tale of the Absurd, or an anti-capital punishment piece? Or something else?

III *a stranger to love, friendship and remorse*

In the first section of this essay, I said that a person who had no values at all would be severely disabled [*this refers to the longer essay from which this is taken - Ed*]. Meursault does value honesty; he won't lie, but are his values enough to qualify him as a person? Remember that Camus is careful to make his hero a stranger who is one of us; Meursault is not on the outside of society through some disability. It is not that he is incapable of understanding the difference between right and wrong. Camus was strongly averse to critics who suggested that Meursault was schizophrenic or a moron. But despite this, there does seem to be something very wrong with the character.

Meursault makes a conscious choice to see the world, and the people in it, the way he does. "When I was a student, I had plenty of that sort of ambition. But when I had to give up my studies, I very soon realized that

---

7   Ibid p.92

8   A reference to Camus's review of Jean-Paul Sartre's *Nausea* in which he writes "A novel is never anything but a philosophy expressed in images. And in a good novel the philosophy has disappeared into the images. But the philosophy need only spill over into the characters and action for it to stick out like a sore thumb, the plot to lose its authenticity, and the novel its life."

none of it really mattered."[9] When his lawyer asks if he felt any grief on the day of his mother's funeral he replies "that [he'd] rather got out of the habit of analysing [himself]"[10]. At his trial, he has an experience that reminds him of the way he used to think, "for the first time in years, I stupidly felt like crying because I could tell how much all these people hated me."[11] At some point in his life, Meursault made his decision not to lie. He stopped analysing himself, and others, and his interactions within society. Personal ambitions, emotions, relationships are, to him, no longer worth thinking about. The question is whether as a result of this decision he ends up as a murderer, deserving Society's hatred.

An unreal crime may be impossible to properly judge. However, Meursault's behaviour and attitude after the event is something we can take into account. The trial is often criticized, as Camus intended, for the focus on Meursault's previous actions and suspected attitudes prior to the shooting rather than on the crime itself.

> "But my lawyer was out of patience and, raising his arms so high that his sleeves fell back to reveal the folds of his starched shirt, he exclaimed, 'But after all, is he being accused of burying his mother or of killing a man?' The public laughed. But the prosecutor rose to his feet again, wrapped his gown about him and announced that only someone as naïve as the honourable counsel for the defence could fail to appreciate that between two such actions there existed a profound, tragic and vital relationship. 'Yes,' he exclaimed vehemently, 'I accuse this man of burying his mother like a heartless criminal.'"[12]

But isn't the problem not that the prosecutor points to events from Meursault's life in order to make judgments about what kind of man he is but that he picks the wrong events? It may not be correct to claim that Meursault is a monster because he didn't cry at his mother's funeral but what about

---

9   Ibid p.44

10   Ibid p.65

11   Ibid p.87

12   Ibid p.93

saying he's a heartless criminal because he unemotionally shot a man and didn't feel remorse for his actions?

The Stranger can be read as a novel about capital punishment and the judicial process. It is also a novel of the Absurd (if not the novel of the Absurd). In this essay I am interested in the Absurd and not whether it is just and right to put Meursault to death. In what follows I will be looking at Meursault's awareness of love, friendship and remorse; or more accurately his lack of awareness.

Patrice Meursault is not a nice man. His sole virtue is a refusal to lie. A virtue he is lacking after his trial. Thinking about the process of killing a condemned man, he says "I imagined that they could find some chemical compound for the patient to take (I thought of him as a patient) which would kill him nine times out of ten."[13] Condemned men are not 'patients' but prisoners. They are not awaiting treatment but (what Society calls) justice. Thinking of himself, and people like him, as patients is hardly a lucid imagining. All of Meursault's thinking while he is in prison is about himself and his life. The life he took does not concern him. At no point after the murder does Meursault show any kind or remorse or regret for killing the Arab. Even as he is stuck in his cell contemplating life and death, and the value of the former, he doesn't think of the life he took from someone else.

During the trial, the prosecutor asks for the death penalty because when he looks at Meursault he sees "nothing but a monster."[14] By contrast the defense lawyer sees a man "popular with everyone and sympathetic to the misfortunes of others."[15] He goes on to say that Meursault is already suffering punishment for his crime, being stricken with "eternal remorse"[16] We know that the defense lawyer is wrong. Far from being stricken with remorse, Meursault was at the time thinking how pointless the whole trial was and wanted simply to return to his cell and go to bed. The defense lawyer was correct, however, when he said that Meursault was popular. He

---

13   Ibid p.106

14   Ibid p.99

15   Ibid p.100

16   Ibid p.101

has a friend at work, Emmanuel, with whom he is close enough to have lunch with and go to the cinema. Marie, his girlfriend, loves him and wants to get married. Raymond is his mate: they go out for drinks, he trusts him with the letter and he likes Meursault enough to invite him to his friend's chalet outside Algiers. Salamano, although not close enough to be called a friend, is on friendly terms with this neighbour. When the old man's dog goes missing, he feels close enough to Meursault to knock on his door for company. Meursault was more than just a customer to Celeste, "yes, but a friend as well."[17] The two of them used to go to the races together on Sundays. With the exception of Emmanuel (who we don't hear of again) all of his friends and acquaintances stand up for him in court. None of them, presumably, consider Meursault to be a stranger, on the outside. Marie thinks he is "peculiar" but "that was probably why she loved [him]"[18]; however, she doesn't think Meursault is disturbed or mentally ill. No-one but the prosecutor does.

He treats Marie quite shockingly; his honesty seems almost cruel. "Marie came round for me and asked if I wanted to marry her. I said I didn't mind and we could if she wanted to. She then wanted to know if I loved her. I replied as I had done once already, that it didn't mean anything but that I probably didn't. 'Why marry me then?' she said. I explained to her that it really didn't matter and that if she wanted to, we could get married. Anyway, she was the one asking and I was simply saying yes. She remarked that marriage was a serious matter. I said 'No'. She didn't say anything for a moment and looked at me in silence."[19]

Meursault may well be being honest with regards to how he feels but certainly doesn't understand the value of love and marriage. His lack of understanding, his inability to appreciate the love someone can offer him, appears to me as a failing, a serious flaw in his character and not a particularly believable one. I can't imagine that Meursault used to understand the importance of loving relationships but one day discovered that they don't matter. For someone to stop appreciating the love of others one would expect them to have suffered a major trauma that precipitates their new outlook. But

---

17   Ibid p.89

18   Ibid p.45

19   Ibid p.44-45

Camus has Meursault say nothing of traumatic events in his past. As far as we can tell, Meursault simply found himself no longer appreciating loving relationships.

Certainly there is some truth in what Meursault says about love but this truth is usually coupled with a contradictory belief that love really does matter. Compare this to what Cherea says about love, death and happiness to Caligula (see below). Love is not rational, for most of us the experience of love is an experience of the Absurd. On the one hand we feel totally committed to the one we love, we treat this love with the utmost importance and believe it will last forever. But on the other hand, we accept that we don't really understand love, and that it usually doesn't last and it never remains the same. Love is impossible to clearly define; however, most of us who have loved and been loved, can recognize the experience of being in love. Something has, and is, occurring when a person is in love; for them it is a real experience, an actual event in the world. Meursault, doesn't feel this and is unaware of it. All he sees is one aspect of what love is and misses another.

What is troubling about Meursault is not so much his one-sided view of love and marriage but his lack of moral concern over how he treats Marie. He knows he doesn't love her but is not concerned that he may be using her simply for the pleasure he can get from her. He even acknowledges that he would get as much pleasure from a similar woman as he does from Marie. His most disturbing thought about Marie is later in prison when it crosses his mind that she might be ill or dead. Rather than feeling concerned he remarks that "I wasn't interested in her anymore if she was dead."[20] It is most shocking when we, like Meursault, forget that he is a criminal in prison for committing an emotionless murder. Such feelings are easier for us to take if they are expressed by a psychopath, a stranger, an outsider.

The lack of concern shown to Marie indicates that he is unaware of how his actions would be received by her. Indeed, throughout the novel he often seems surprised by the reaction of others. For instance, when he displays no remorse over the murder of the Arab, he can't understand why the

---

20   Ibid p.110

prosecutor "was so furious about it"[21] Even if Meursault had come to realize that others in Society don't tell the truth and don't refuse to lie, he ought to be aware of how they would experience him especially since before he stopped analysing the world he used to be like everyone else.

His friendship with Raymond is odd. He appears to start the friendship simply because his neighbour offers food, "I realized that this would save me having to cook for myself and I accepted."[22] Raymond offers friendship and Meursault takes it but without offering friendship in return. Raymond would be unaware of course that his new 'friend' is not offering any friendship back because Meursault certainly appears to. He helps him with the problem of dealing with his mistress, by not judging him over the beating and agreeing that it was the right thing to do, and by writing the letter. He also goes out drinking with Raymond and, of course, goes to the beach with him that crucial Sunday. If Meursault really were truthful, then he would be aware that he wasn't actually friends with Raymond and would not continue deceiving him by letting him think otherwise. But then again, Meursault may not be aware of this because he has given up analyzing his actions.

When he writes the letter for Raymond, he does so "to please Raymond but because [he] had no reason not to please him"[23] A good reason not to please him would be the sense that helping orchestrate the physical and emotional abuse of a girl he has never met is morally wrong. But Meursault doesn't care about what is right and what is wrong. But what reason does Meursault have to please Raymond? The only answer in the text seems to be that he finds Raymond's stories interesting[24] and that if he didn't please the man then presumably he wouldn't get to hear them any more. Unlike Raymond, Meursault doesn't consider them both to be friends. Rather, Raymond is at best a interesting distraction for him. After his outburst in prison to the priest, Meursault says "What did it matter that Raymond was just as much my mate as Celeste who was worth more than him?"[25] As with

---

21   Ibid p.97

22   Ibid p.32

23   Ibid p.38

24   Ibid p.32

25   Ibid p.116

love, Meursault does not value friendship. And this appears to be because Meursault is not experiencing friendship. Instead he simply looks and acts like a friend, does a passable impression, without actually being a friend.

The most troubling thing about Meursault is his lack of remorse over the killing of the Arab and his lack of understanding that some expression of regret is expected by others. He finds it difficult to accept that he has committed a crime and is a criminal. He admits to not being able to take the examining magistrate seriously. "On my way out I was even going to shake his hand, but I remembered just in time that I'd killed a man."[26] On a later occasion he feels a bit frightened by the magistrate but "realized at the same time that this is ridiculous because, after all, I was the criminal."[27] I have already mentioned above how Meursault in prison doesn't see himself as a prisoner guilty of murder awaiting execution but as a patient awaiting some kind of procedure. When asked outright if he regrets what he's done, his reply: "I thought it over and said that, rather than true regret, I felt a kind of annoyance."[28]

Meursault is not seen as strange or an outsider by the people who know him. We have seen that they like him, enjoy his company and consider him to be a man of the world (as opposed to a stranger to the world?). But this is because they mistakenly assume him to be capable of love and friendship. He doesn't see himself as a stranger either. A most telling statement by him on the subject occurs when he reflects on a meeting with his lawyer, "I wanted to assure him that I was just like everyone else, exactly like everyone else. But it was all really a bit pointless and I couldn't be bothered."[29] How could Meursault make a choice to be different, to stop analysing life, to cease appreciating love and friendship and to be unable to feel either horror or remorse over the killing of another man and then think he's just like everyone else?

---

26   Ibid p.64

27   Ibid p.68

28   Ibid p.69

29   Ibid p.66

Meursault appears to be completely unaware of those aspects of love, friendship, and justice that are not rational. The experience of being in love, of having friendships with others, of justice is completely alien to him. As a result, Meursault is incapable of sharing these things with other members of his society. He is a pure individual with no sense of solidarity with others. In this sense he is an outsider. He can not identify with us and we can not identify with him. He is a stranger.

IV *thought experiments*

Consider the following: I can rationally argue that once a human being is dead they can suffer no harm to their body. In fact, I can argue that once a person is dead, they no longer have a body. Pointing to a cadaver, how can I say it *belongs* to a dead person? Yet despite knowing this, if someone I am eating dinner with suddenly drops dead to the floor, I would feel it to be morally wrong to put 'their' hand under the table leg to stop the table wobbling; or to roll the body against the door to prevent a draught coming in. You wouldn't believe it if someone claimed that they did such a thing because they accepted the rational truth that the deceased was not harmed by the body being used as a draught excluder. You wouldn't expect to be able to persuade an otherwise rational person to use the body of a recently deceased person in such a way. We know that rational argument has never been so successful as to prevent such a strong emotional response from taking precedence. In fact I am inclined to believe that a person, who on the strength of rational argument, can use a dead body to temporarily stop a table from wobbling simply doesn't understand the full reality of the situation.

A less extreme thought experiment will be helpful. When someone close to you dies it is natural to suffer grief. It is very painful at first and then this initial grief becomes less acute and we can start to remember the person we've lost without feeling intense pain. Imagine that a woman in her late thirties loses her husband in an accident. She feels terrible, intense, grief and suffering. However, rationally, she is aware that (a) in thirty years time she won't feel so bad and (b) her husband wouldn't want her to suffer. She can imagine herself sitting on a beach in thirty years time, with a new man she meets ten years from now. They have been married for twenty years and are on holiday celebrating their retirement and looking forward to spending their twilight years together. She looks at her second husband and feels the warmth of her love for him. She remembers her first husband and how much she loved him too. At this moment she realizes that it is truly possible to lose someone you love and love someone else without pain and contradiction. Now if it were medically possible to create a pill that would eliminate the intense pain the woman feels when loss of her husband is fresh and raw and replace it with the feeling she has thirty years later, should she take it? Why would she want to?

There is a sense that it would be wrong to avoid the pain and suffering of grief. What a person feels when the bereavement is fresh and what they feel years later is just as true. However, without feeling the former it seems impossible for someone to experience the latter. That is, if a person didn't feel intense loss it is difficult to accept that they felt intense love. The pill medically removes the 'early' feelings and replaces them with the 'later' ones but someone taking this pill will not be feeling emotions they ought to feel now and will feel emotions they shouldn't be feeling yet. Creating such a pill in real life is impossible. Just as impossible would be someone, when newly bereaved, choosing to experience the 'later' emotions.

Suppose you bumped into a friend whose partner had recently died but he appeared bright and cheery. When you inquire after his good mood he claims that his partner asked him not to suffer grief after her death and he's honouring her wishes. You simply would not be able to believe that he chose not to suffer. Either he is putting on an elaborate show of not feeling the grief he does, or, more likely, he didn't actually love his wife and genuinely doesn't grieve her passing.

Someone who doesn't grieve after the loss of a loved one never had a loved one. Without the appropriate emotional response one can not understand the truth of certain things in the world. Loving someone, being friends with someone, requires an emotional understanding of what love and friendship is. When someone has the wrong emotional reaction to an event we assume, correctly I think, that they don't understand what is going on. If a child runs out into the road and is run over and killed, even if the driver could have done nothing to prevent it, if they are completely blameless, we will still expect them to feel some kind of guilt. If the driver had the same emotional response to the tragic accident as someone else, who merely read about it in the paper, we would think there was something wrong with the driver's understanding of events. Although, I believe, it can not be rationally argued why the driver should feel worse than the newspaper reader.

If a friend of yours was in this situation; was suffering from terrible guilt and you told them not to feel guilty, that there was nothing they could have done, you wouldn't believe that they could simply choose to stop feeling guilty. If they did, you would think something was wrong with them, even though they were following your advice.

A final example. Imagine a man who worries every time his wife or child travels home alone at night on their own. He learns that a pharmaceutical company has developed a pill that will replace this worry with the worry similar to that a person feels at the idea of women and children in general traveling alone at night. He buys some of these pills and the next time his wife tells him that she'll be coming home late on her own he takes one. His worry for her in particular is reduced to a lesser concern for women traveling home late at night in general. The pill works a treat and he spends a comfortable night at home. A few months later he discovers that the pharmaceutical company has developed more pills. There is one that replaces the worry that his family are happy with the worry that the family across the street are happy. Another that replaces the feeling one gets when learning of a disaster that occurred in a town nearby with one that has happened on the other side of the world. They even have a pill in development that will remove all feelings of ambition and there's a suggestion of a pill that can replace a feeling of revulsion in the face of injustice with cool indifference.

I doubt whether someone who took these pills would continue to be a fully functioning person. I am certain that no-one could simply choose to replace these feelings. They could think about their wives in a different way, stop caring about her as a person and lose concern for her traveling home alone on her own. However, no-one could love someone just as much as ever but simply choose to not be concerned for their welfare in certain situations they now to be dangerous. Not, convince themselves that the situations are not dangerous, but simply choose not be concerned.

According to Camus, Meursault used to understand the world in the same way most of us do but then he chose to understand it differently. It simply isn't believable that such a decision is possible. One would expect a person who was capable but is now *incapable* of being in love, experiencing friendship or feeling remorse after causing the death of another, to have undergone some terrible trauma that precipitated the change (Caligula and the loss of Drusilla). Or a long chronic unhappiness that slowly destroys the person they used to be (Martha and her need to escape to the sun). However, Camus can not have his hero be an outsider because he is disabled or suffering from a mental illness. He wants us to see Meursault's point of view as a legitimate choice not as the ravings of a man deranged (and therefore easy to dismiss). In *The* Stranger Meursault suffers no trauma (except at the end) but makes a choice instead. A choice I don't think a person can realistically make which is why I claim Meursault is a unreal character. And his story, unreal also. In the next section I will explore the idea that Meursault is a human without human nature.

V *Meursault may be unreal but he is not absurd*

There are two ways of looking at such things as love, friendship, and morality. We can look at these things rationally and discover 'truths' that we don't appreciate. For example, with morality, we can discover that although we treat our moral decisions with the utmost seriousness they rest on arbitrarily chosen beliefs. How can we continue to take such beliefs seriously? We could, like Meursault, stop taking them seriously (that is if it is under our control to do so). However, if we don't, if we continue to take our moral beliefs seriously despite being aware of the arbitrary nature of them, then we are absurd.

Most people do not look at such things as love, friendship, and morality lucidly. Rather than facing up the arbitrariness of things, they simply assume that these things are founded in fundamental rational truths that justify them. They continue to treat them with the utmost seriousness and believe that it is normal and right to do so. As we shall see below, they are like Cherea in *Caligula* avoiding looking too deeply because they want to live and be happy. However, when we do so, we miss something. Like Meursault we are unaware of the whole picture but the bit we don't see is the only thing Meursault does see. The Absurd involves a clash of two conflicting beliefs. If we arbitrarily label these beliefs (a) and (b), we can say that while most of us are only aware of (a), Meursault is only aware of (b).

To be absurd, one would need to be totally lucid, aware of both (a) and (b). Thus, since Meursault is only aware of one, he is not absurd.

VI *emotion, sentiment, human nature and the Absurd*

In *The Rebel* Camus recognizes rebellion as beginning with an emotional reaction to injustice.

> "In every act of rebellion, the man concerned experiences not only a feeling of revulsion at the infringement of his rights but also a complete and spontaneous loyalty to certain aspects of himself."[30]

When someone rebels, becomes a rebel, she "tacitly invokes a value."[31] This comes about suddenly when confronted with an injustice (either suffered by the rebel personally or witnessed as the suffering of others). When this feeling of revulsion at injustice occurs and a person feels what Camus calls an "awakening of conscience" there is a value created "with which the rebel can identify himself – even if only for a moment."[32] There is no period of reflection; that, if it comes at all, comes later. All the individual is aware of is a confused feeling that there is something they value and that it has been violated. Camus refers to this aspect of a person, this spontaneous emotional response to injustice, as "the passionate side of his nature that serves no other purpose but to help him to live."[33] For Camus, unlike his existentialist contemporaries, analysis of this kind of rebellion "leads us to the suspicion that, contrary to the postulates of contemporary thought, a human nature does exist, as the Greeks believed. Why rebel if there is nothing worth preserving in oneself?"[34] Indeed, it is this part of human nature that Camus asserts "must always be defended."[35] How unlike the attitude of his character Meursault.

30   Albert Camus, *The Rebel* (Penguin 2000) p.19

31   Ibid p.20

32   Ibid

33   Ibid p.25

34   Ibid p.22

35   Ibid p.25

Or that of Martha, from his play *Cross Purpose*. Let's take a look at Meursault's speech made during his outburst to the priest.

> "I'd been right, I was still right, I was always right. I'd lived a certain way and I could just as well lived a different way. I'd done this and I hadn't done that. I hadn't done one thing whereas I had done another. So what? It was as if I'd been waiting all along for this very moment and for the early dawn when I'd be justified. Nothing, nothing mattered and I knew very well why. [The priest] too knew why. From the depths of my future, throughout the whole absurd life I'd been leading, I'd felt a vague breath drifting towards me across all the years that were still to come, and on its way this breath had evened out everything that was being proposed to me in the equally unreal years I was living through. What did other people's deaths or a mother's love matter to me, what did his God or the lives people chose or the destinies they selected matter to me, when one and the same destiny was to select me and thousands of millions of other privileged people who, like him, called themselves my brothers. Didn't he understand? Everyone was privileged. There were only privileged people. The others too would be condemned one day. He too would be condemned. What did it matter if he was accused of murder and then executed for not crying at his mother's funeral?"[36]

Now let's compare this murderer's speech with another's, Martha. In the third act of *Cross Purpose*, Martha, the sister of Jan, whom she has murdered in order to steal his money, is confronted by Maria, Jan's wife.

> "MARIA [*in a sort of reverie*]: But why, *why* did you do it?
>
> MARTHA: What right do you have to question me?
>
> MARIA [*passionately*]: What right?... My love for him.
>
> MARTHA: What does that word mean?

---

36   Albert Camus, *The Outsider* (Penguin 1983) p.115-116

MARIA: It means – it means all that at this moment is tearing, gnawing at my heart; it means this rush of frenzy that makes my fingers itch for murder. It means all my past joys, and this wild, sudden grief you have brought me. Yes, you crazy woman, if it wasn't that I've steeled my heart against believing, you'd learn the meaning of that word, when you felt my nails scoring your cheeks.

MARTHA: Again you are using language I cannot understand. Words like love and joy and grief are meaningless to me.

MARIA [*making a great effort to speak calmly*]: Listen, Martha – that's your name isn't it? Let's stop this game, if game it is, of cross-purposes. Let's have done with useless words. Tell me quite clearly what I want to know quite clearly before I let myself break down.

MARTHA: Surely I made it clear enough. We did to your husband last night what we had done to other travelers, before; we killed him and took his money.

MARIA: So his mother and sister were criminals?

MARTHA: Yes. But that's their business, and no one else's."[37]

Martha is different to Meursault in that she took people's lives deliberately and with a purpose. The deaths were necessary so that the men could be robbed and Martha and her mother would have enough money to escape to the sea. Certainly, Martha feels no malice towards her victims, except for Jan when he humanizes himself, making it harder to murder him without conscience. She seems to have steeled herself against weakness, in order to be able to do what she needs to do to get what she wants. Meursault, as we have seen, simply made a choice to be the way he is and has no ambition. When Martha's mother doesn't show her the love she believes she deserves, Martha is distraught.

---

37   Albert Camus, *Cross Purpose*, Albert Camus: Caligula and other plays (Penguin 2006) p.157

"MARTHA [*burying her face in her* hands]: But what, oh what can mean more to you than your daughter's grief?

THE MOTHER: Weariness, perhaps... and my longing for rest."[38]

Meursault on the other hand cares little for his mother's love. He did his duty by her, or didn't, depending on your attitude to putting relatives in care homes and proper funeral etiquette. What the two killers have in common is that they fail to recognize the value of others. They are pure individuals (Martha wants to take her mother away with her but not for her mother's sake) and can not think in terms of how their lives impact others and vice-versa. One would have thought that even a killer would be able to understand that the wife of their victim can expect an explanation. Or that people in a court-room would want to know why a man was killed and what the killer thought about his actions. Both Martha and Meursault are outsiders because they have no sense of the solidarity that the rest of us value.

A third outsider is Caligula. *Caligula* was written around the same time as *The Stranger* and performed within a year of *Cross Purpose*. Both plays were published along side each other in 1944, a couple of years after the 1942 publications of *The Stranger* and *The Myth of Sisyphus*. In order to understand what Camus is trying to do with his character Meursault, we need to compare him (Meursault) with his contemporaries, Martha and Caligula.

Caligula, after the death of Drusilla, wants solitude. He is overcome with grief (after a trauma, unlike Meursault) and is haunted by thoughts of his past and concerns about his impending future. These future concerns are not about ambition, he is, after all, the most powerful man in Rome. Sick with the world and things in the world, he tells Helicon, his friend, that what he wants is the moon. "Really, this world of ours, the scheme of things as they call it, is quite intolerable. That's why I want the moon, or happiness, or eternal life – something, in fact, that may sound crazy but isn't of this

---

38   Ibid. p.153

world,"[39] However, he knows that getting his hands on the moon is impossible and so he seeks escape from the world. He goes about his escape in two ways. Firstly, he escapes from other people by living outside of human solidarity. Secondly, he is well aware that this choice will ultimately end in his death. It is first his mind, then his body, that will be leaving the world. In an argument with Scipio at the end of the second act, the boy expresses his pity (as well as his hatred) for Caligula and the loneliness he must feel. Caligula fires back:

> "Loneliness! What do *you* know of it? Only the loneliness of poets and weaklings. You prate of loneliness, but you don't realize that one is *never* alone. Always we are attended by the same load of the future and the past. Those we have killed are always with us. But *they* are no great trouble. It's those we have loved, those who have loved us and whom we did not love; regrets, desires, bitterness and sweetness, whores and gods, the gang celestial! Always, always with us! [*He releases Scipio and moves back to his former place.*] Alone! Ah, if only in this loneliness, this ghoul-haunted wilderness of mine, I could know, but for a moment, real solitude, real silence, the throbbing stillness of a tree! [*sitting down, in an excess of fatigue*] Solitude? No Scipio, mine is full of the gnashings of teeth, hideous with jarring sounds and voices. And when I am with the women I make mine and darkness falls on us and I think, now my body's had its fill, that I can feel myself my own at last poised between death and life – ah, then my solitude is fouled by the stale smell of pleasure from the woman sprawling at my side."[40]

Caligula talks again of his 'glorious isolation' as he strangles to death his mistress Caesonia. but before we come to that, it will be helpful to look at the exchange between Caligula and Cherea at the end of Act Three. The emperor has called in Cherea in order to have a frank exchange of ideas. This clash of ideas will result in death; while Caligula obviously has the power to have the other man killed on the spot, Cherea can, and will, plot the assassination of the emperor. We join the discussion just after Cherea has told Caligula why he wants him dead. Caligula pushes him to say more:

---

39   Albert Camus, *Caligula*, Albert Camus: Caligula and other plays (Penguin 2006) p.40

40   Ibid p.68-69

"CHEREA: There's no more to say. I'll be no party to your logic. I've a very different notion of my duties as a man. And I know that the majority of your subjects share my view. You outrage their deepest feelings. It's only natural that you should... disappear.

CALIGULA: I see your point, and it's legitimate enough. For most men I grant you, it's obvious. But *you*, I should have thought, would have known better. You're an intelligent man, and given intelligence, one has a choice: either to pay its price or disown it. Why do you shirk the issue and neither disown it or consent to pay its price?

CHEREA: Because what I want is to live, and to be happy. Neither, to my mind, is possible if one pushes the absurd to its logical conclusions. As you see, I'm quite an ordinary sort of man. True, there are moments when, to feel free of them, I desire the death of those I love, or I hanker after women from whom the ties of family or friendship debar me. Were logic everything, I'd kill or fornicate on such occasions. But I consider that these passing fancies have no great importance. If everyone set to gratifying them, the world would be impossible to live in, and happiness, too, would go by the board. And these, I repeat, are the things that count, for me.

CALIGULA: So, I take it, you believe in some higher principle?

CHEREA: Certainly I believe that some actions are – shall I say? – more praiseworthy than others.

CALIGULA: And *I* believe that all are on an equal footing."[41]

Cherea points out the effect of outrage Caligula's injustice has on the ordinary people. They are revolted by him and will want him dead. Caligula agrees but he thinks a man of Cherea's intelligence should be able to rise above this sentimental, emotional reaction. Unlike Caligula, Cherea can categorize things in the world into good and bad, rankings in order of moral

---

41   Ibid p82-83

preference, and so on. What he shares with Caligula is that he can not find a logical reason to defend his choices. The only reason he makes them is because he wants to live and be happy. Caligula, on the other hand, wants neither. There is no logical reason Caligula can find for killing or not killing; doing this action or that; all are on an equal footing: the very approach to the world that Meursault takes. However, unlike Meursault, Caligula is aware of that spark of human nature that is sentiment, emotion. Which is why Caligula is unhappy and Meursault isn't. Let's explore this idea more closely.

Caligula, just before strangling his mistress to death, claims that he *is* happy. He has discovered that "beyond the frontier of pain lies a splendid, sterile happiness." Once he discovered that nothing lasts, once he is free of illusion, free of memories of the past and thoughts for the future he is finally free. Exclaiming this with bitter laughter he says, "there have been just two or three of us in history who really achieved this freedom, this crazy happiness [...] But for this freedom I'd have been a contented man. Thanks to it, I have won a godlike enlightenment of the solitary [...] And this, *this* is happiness; this and nothing else – this intolerable release, devastating scorn, blood and hatred all around me; the glorious isolation of a man who all his life long nurses and gloats over the joy ineffable of the unpunished murderer; the ruthless logic that crushes out human lives [*he laughs*]"[42]

His happiness is false. Happy people don't laugh bitterly, nor do they describe their feelings as 'sterile'. Caligula refers to 'this crazy happiness'. He recognizes that all is possibly not well and that he is not happy. As he squeezes the life out of Caesonia he says, "No. No sentiment. I must have done with it, for the time is short. My time is very short, dear Caesonia."[43] Is he talking to her or himself when he calls out for no sentiment. No sentiment as he kills his 'dear Caesonia'. Moments later, when he knows his assassins are coming and that his plans have worked – worked in the sense that men are coming to take him out of the world – he calls out "I have chosen the wrong path, a path that leads to nothing. My freedom isn't the right one..."[44]

---

42   Ibid p.102

43   Ibid

44   ibid p.103

Now let us compare Caligula's 'sterile happiness' with Martha's desire to escape somewhere where the sun burns everything up.

> "MARTHA: I read in a book that it even burns out people's soul and gives them bodies that shine like gold but are quite hollow, there's nothing left inside.

> THE MOTHER: Is that what makes you want to go there so much?

> MARTHA: Yes, my soul's a burden to me, I've had enough of it. I'm eager to be in that country, where the sun kills every question. I don't belong here."[45]

Like Caligula, Martha is seeking a sterile happiness, hers to be sterilized by the heat of the sun. She wants to escape all questions and live a life plagued by none. Like Caligula, she appears to be bothered by sentiment. She does everything she can to avoid getting intimate with Jan. Ironically, it is during a intimate conversation with her brother that she makes up her mind to kill him. Rather than thinking things through with cold logic and choosing the rational answer, she is motivated by her emotional desire to step foot on the scorching beaches of the coast. Her and her mother also rationalize their murders, making out that they are in fact doing their victims a favour. The murdered guests are drugged beforehand and neither predict nor suffer their actual deaths. This, to Martha and her mother, makes their victims fortunate and hides the horror behind the reality of their actions. Sentiment is acknowledged and overcome with philosophy.

Caligula and Martha are much more believable characters than Meursault. They are both human, and feel human emotions. Sure, they devise strategies to overcome human nature but this proves that they are more aware, more lucid of events, than Meursault who appears to be without human nature. What I mean by overcoming human nature is managing to suppress the feeling of sentiment that rises in the face of injustice as well as similar emotions that appear when confronted with love and friendship. Note

---

45   Albert Camus, *Cross Purpose*, Albert Camus: Caligula and other plays (Penguin 2006) p.111

that both Caligula and Martha want a sterile happiness, purged of emotion and sentiment. You don't want to be purged of something you don't have.

The other people around Caligula and Martha recognize their madness. Although it is not the politically correct term by today's standard, we know what Maria means when she says Martha is crazy. The patricians understand that Caligula is beside himself. Cherea makes a point of not hating him because he doesn't think Caligula is happy. He recognizes that the man is "noxious and cruel, vain and selfish"[46] Obviously, he is aware that Caligula has these negative qualities but does not blame him for them; he can not hate the man even though he knows he is noxious and cruel. Why? Because he doesn't think it is Caligula's fault; he believes Caligula to be beside himself with grief over the death of Drusilla. It is easy to see Caligula and Martha as different because in their effort to suppress their emotions, in order to overcome the Absurd, they come across to others as mad. Meursault doesn't appear mad (until he is questioned about the murder of the Arab then he only comes across as mad because he seems so unaffected by his actions) because Meursault isn't tormented by a confrontation with the Absurd. He can not look at the world and his place in it lucidly because he is blind to the understanding human emotion gives us. Thus there is no clash, no conflict, and nothing is absurd.

Unlike Meursault, Caligula and Martha experience and understand the world through emotion: grief, anger, scorn, longing, despair. They develop strategies to overcome their human instincts and end up in isolation, murder and death. Meursault is also isolated but does not have the same understanding of the world as the other two because he is incapable of experiencing the world around him and the people in it emotionally. More accurately, he is not entirely emotionless, he has no reason to lie when he says (to Salamano and us, the readers) that he is upset about the dog going missing. The emotions he is lacking in are what is needed to desire and feel solidarity with others. The emotions that, according to Camus, make being human beings what they are. In *The Rebel*, he observes that rebellion (an emotional response to injustice) is "the common ground on which every man bases his first values. I *rebel* – therefore we *exist*."[47]

---

46   Albert Camus, *Caligula*, Albert Camus: Caligula and other plays (Penguin 2006) p.82

47   Albert Camus, *The Rebel* (Penguin 2000) p.28

It is interesting to note that in his cell Meursault discovers a scrap of newspaper on which he can read a report of a crime very similar to Martha's. There are slight differences: in the news report the son is beaten to death with a hammer rather than drugged, the mother hangs herself rather than drowns herself and the Martha character throws herself down a well. Meursault comments, "I must have read this story thousands of times. On the one hand, it was quite improbable. On the other, it was quite natural. Anyway, I decided that the traveller had deserved it really and that you should never play around."[48] He might not have an emotional connection to Martha and her crime, but there is something like sympathy for her situation.

Conclusion

Camus was averse to any criticism of Meursault's humanity. He claims that Meursault is a passionate man who refuses to lie. And because he refuses to lie, to say more than what he feels in his heart, society feels threatened. It is Meursault "who agrees to die for the truth."[49] I have already mentioned in my introduction that Camus considers his character to be Christ-like. Perhaps when he refers to Meursault's passion, it is in terms of his sufferings as a martyr – dying, as Camus claims he does, for the truth. But dying because you refuse to lie is not the same thing as dying *for* the truth. And Meursault does not agree to die but at best simply goes along with it. Society doesn't kill him because it is threatened by his refusal to lie but because he killed a fellow man in cold blood. For sure, Meursault won't lie and say that he feels guilt or remorse when he only feels a sense of annoyance and it is this that probably seals his fate in court. However, he is not condemned simply because he refuses to say more than he feels or because he will only tell the truth – if that were so, simply telling the truth, no matter what the content of that truth happens to be, would be a capital offence. The truth is that he is a remorseless killer. Yes, everything is simple. It is Camus who complicates things. Don't let him say about the man condemned to death: "He is put to

---

48   Albert Camus, *The Outsider* (Penguin 1983) p.78

49 Albert Camus, *Afterword*, The Outsider (Penguin 1983) p.119

death because he didn't cry at his mother's funeral," but: "They're going to chop his head off." It may seem like nothing. But it does make a difference.[50]

So far, I have mentioned Caligula's acute crisis, the death of Drusilla, that brings about in him a lucidity of the Absurd. I have mentioned Martha's chronic isolation and resentment that allows her to be lucid of the Absurd. But I have not mentioned Meursault's realization, in the last few pages of the novel, of why his mother chose to take a fiancé when she was so close to death. I wonder if it would have made a difference to me, as the reader, if he had awoken in his cell and realized why he didn't deserve crowds of spectators crying their hatred at his execution. Not due to his innocence but because it seems more just that his death be met with the same indifference he feels toward the man he killed.

The Stranger is an uncomfortable read and Meursault an incomprehensible character. The Absurd arises in a moment of lucidity, when we are aware of a clash between two conflicting beliefs. The world seems absurd because we are part of nature and yet able to take a step back from nature and rationalize our place in the world. We become aware of what we call the Absurd when we can not reconcile the two experiences: what we instinctively feel to be true and what we rationally believe to be true. In *The Rebel* Camus looks to human nature to make sense of what we are to do about the problem. The hero of his novel of the Absurd, arguably *the novel of the Absurd*, doesn't have a problem with it. If he had had a cold that fateful Sunday and stayed at home, then the killing would never have happened and he would presumably live the rest of his life untroubled by the Absurd – or the rest of society. Caligula and Martha struggle with their confrontation but they are more human, more real, than Meursault. *The Stranger* gives the reader the sense of confusion and isolation one feels when looking for meaning, in, what very well could be, a meaningless universe. However, *Caligula* and *Cross Purpose* give us a better understanding of the Absurd.

---

[50] See *Between Yes and No* in The Wrong Side and The Right Side. Camus says "I need my lucidity. Yes, everything is simple. It's men who complicate things. Don't let them tell us any stories. Don't let them say about a man condemned to death: "He is going to pay his debt to society," but: "They're going to chop his head off." It may seem like nothing. But it does make a difference. There are some people who like to look their destiny straight in the eye.

Camus and the Absurd Cycle

By Peter Francev

Albert Camus was one of the most diverse thinker-writers to emerge out of post-World War II France. Not only did he dabble in his first love - the theatre - but Camus was awarded the Nobel Prize for literature in 1957 for his body of fiction that is infused with the quintessentially existential theory of the Absurd. While the roots of the Absurd grew out of the 19th century Russian nihilism of Ivan Turgenev and Fyodor Dostoevsky, and the elaboration of Nietzsche, it was Camus who became the first philosopher to examine the Absurd as an independent extension of nihilism. Ultimately, Camus had envisioned what he dubbed "the Absurd Cycle". Ideally, this would consist of a dramatic work, a work of fiction - namely a novel - and a theoretical work that would philosophically detail the three particular aspects of the Absurd Cycle - freedom, revolt and passion.

Camus was able to complete the first two cycles of the Absurd named: "Absurd Freedom" and "Absurd Revolt"; he had planned to finish the cycle with "Absurd Passion", yet his untimely death precluded its completion. The purpose of this paper is to examine the intricacies of the Absurd Cycle - mainly that of the evolution of *The Rebel* from *The Myth of Sisyphus* (henceforth, *The Myth*) - and illustrate a justification for the Absurd Cycle's completion beyond freedom and revolt. However, before this can be accomplished, the background of nihilism's transformation to the Absurd must be established in order to provide a sound basis for the paper.

Turgenev was nihilism's proponent, and he was the first person to refer to the new word as a proper term yet he failed to go into detail on any kind of specific definition. He leaves the terms as a rather open-ended idea (that is to say that just the term is given and without any explanation) in his 1862 novel *Fathers and Sons*. This is to say that Turgenev's contemporary, Dostoevsky, elaborates on nihilism in terms of the character in: *Notes from Underground, Crime and Punishment, The Possessed* and *The Brothers Karamazov*. Like Turgenev, Dostoevsky never quite establishes a formal definition or analysis of nihilism, in every case, his characters move seemingly through the novels without any kind of metamorphosis away their nihilistic states of being. They just exist as is - nihilistic beings. For example, just by reading Dostoevsky's first "major" novels - *Notes From Underground* - students of the Russian novelist encounter the unnamed protagonist "Underground" whose nihilistic sense of self permeates through the course of the sixteen-year time-frame of the novel as well as a university dropout who subsists on the fringes of society as a social phantom.

The novel begins with a dejected and bitter unnamed protagonist, here referred to as "Underground Man", prophesizing about how it is "rude", "indecent", and "immoral"[51] to live one's life beyond the age of 40; ironically, he, too, is 40 years of age. Also, he continues his nihilistic discourse by stating that while employed as a government official, he had the power to approve and disapprove of individuals seeking permit acceptance. Routinely Underground states that he "took pleasure"[52] in anguishing those seeking his permission and, in doing so, he is able to project his misery onto others. It is only when he elicits a negative response from his clients that he feels a sense of empowerment, which, ultimately, nullifies his feelings of the Absurd.

In his second major novel, *Crime and* Punishment, Raskolnikov, the protagonist in *Crime and Punishment*, is a bit more complex than his forerunner. He commits a seemingly selfish and heartless double-murder of the local pawnbroker and her sister, who unintentionally and unfortunately witnesses the former's initial murder. Yet, midway through the novel an ethical - and almost honorable - side emerges when he decides to spend what little money he possesses on the wake and funeral of the neighborhood drunk. Grateful for his monetary - and emotional - support, Raskolnikov is befriended by the deceased man's 20 year-old daughter Sonya. Over the course of the last half of the novel Sonya and her devout Russian Orthodoxy ebbs and flows with Raskolnikov's apathetic and religious indifference, ultimately culminating in the last scene of the novel, and which also appears to be Raskolnikov's "Lazarus" moment, in which he seems to be awaken from the "unethical dead" as he picks up Sonya's copy of the New Testament.

---

[51] *NFU* (4)

[52] *NFU* (3)

While Dostoevsky never acknowledges Raskolnikov's conversion, readers are left wondering "What if?" and "Does he convert? If not to Christianity, then does he undergo a kind of anti-nihilistic salvation?" ultimately, this leaves readers feeling that all that can be assumed is: Raskolnikov remains as nihilistic at the end of the novel as he is at its beginning.

Nietzsche's interest in the nihilism stems from having been influenced directly by Dostoevsky; and he discusses nihilism in the most negative of terms: one where "Everything lacks meaning"[53]. It is in Book One of his posthumous work *The Will to Power* that Nietzsche criticizes a very decadent European society in which "man has lost the faith in his own value when no infinitely valuable whole works through him."[54] [...] "The Germans of today are no thinkers any longer: something else delights and impresses them."[55] Ironically, while using nihilism as a generalization for European society, the term "nihilism" metamorphoses into what is seen as Nietzsche's specific critique of German society. In his youth, Nietzsche idolized the "perfection" of the German people and their culture; now, it seems as if that embodiment of magnificence and its glorification have been annihilated by its greatest proponent because of its apparent decadence.

Nietzsche is the first philosopher to theorize nihilism, which includes a critique of society rather than just the individual. Unrecognized for some forty years, Camus is the first contemporary thinker to elucidate on nihilism. This would evolve into what would become his philosophy of the Absurd. For Camus, it is the question of suicide that is the most basic tenet of the absurd and the most fundamental problem of philosophical questioning.

Before examining *The Rebel*, the Absurd needs to be elaborated in *The Myth* in order to set up the framework that provides the foundation that Camus goes into detail in *The Rebel* itself. *The Myth* opens with there being

---

[53] Nietzsche, *WP*, 7

[54] Ibid, 12

[55] Ibid, xxiii

"one truly serious philosophical problem, and that is suicide. Judging whether life is or is not worth living amounts to answering the fundamental question of philosophy." (3) Individuals are faced with a perplexing dualism: either commit suicide or live in the face of the Absurd as absurd and positively move forward with acceptance.

As it was for Hamlet and countless other characters - both fictional and non-fictional, "to be, or not to be" is the beginning of all philosophical questioning. It is the point of departure in the inquiry of meaningfulness of life, and thoughts of suicide, invariably, lead to anxiety. According to Stephen Bronner, "suicide is an expression of the absurd...."[56] If an individual, confronted with the Absurd, commits suicide, then the act of suicide becomes an admission that life is: a) worthless, and/or b) too difficult to encounter which produces the Absurd. Thus, for the individual who chooses not to commit suicide by choosing to live, the meaninglessness of life is negated and the individual is able to move forward - away from the Absurdity of suicide. It is at this point that the individual is on the path towards meaning.

Once an individual has determined that life is worth living and that suicide is not a viable option, that person is prepared to move forward because "everything begins with consciousness."[57] Conscious recognition is the starting point where the individual chooses to examine his life. By questioning the validity of life, a confrontation has occurred; one where the moment of precise recognition in an alien world cannot be ignored. It is at this moment that the individual — the soon to-be rebel - is faced with one of three types of Absurd Man.

According to Camus, once the individual has chosen life, there are three possible classes of Absurd Man that the individual can be categorized into: the Don Juan, the actor, or the conqueror. If a person is a type of Don Juan, then he "sees nothing but justification" in others and he has nothing to justify.[58] This is to say that while the Don Juan is objectifying his victims, his

---

[56] Bronner (46)

[57] Camus, *MS*, 13.

[58] Ibid, 67.

life is one of absurdity. Sure, he does not think about his victims, the immorality of his actions, or the objectification of the women that he seduces. He does not hope to find the "perfect" mate, or even a wife for that matter; he does not even "aim to please", just merely find another "conquest" for the night. There is an emptiness that precludes his search for meaning in the conquests for the nights ahead. And while a small contingency of thinkers might be inclined to argue that since Don Juan is advantageously seeking another subjugation - and that there is meaningfulness in that quest - the pursuit and pursuantee become a means to an end which happens to re-cycle each day and night and provide a meaninglessness to his existence.

On the other hand, the second type of "rebel" is the actor, who is an absurd character because his world - the world of fantasy and make-believe — is fleeting. When the actor steps onto the stage, in front of an audience or camera, his "real" identity is destroyed—even if only temporarily—and he assumes the new persona of the character with which he is invested to portray. The actor lives a kind of "double life" where, even if only briefly, he is able to assume the identity of the character that he portrays; thus, he provides himself with an imagined life that is not necessarily his. Excellent actors, those who are universally recognized as "great" actors, are those who can lure, through their acting skills, the audience into their roles and momentarily suspend identification of their "real" life. For example, is Lawrence Olivier a great (or arguably the greatest) Shakespearean actor because of the quantity of roles that he has endured, or because when we see a cinematic version of *Hamlet*, we are entranced by the quality of his performance and find ourselves sympathizing with the fictional character's plight?

While the actor is able to live two lives simultaneously, the conqueror, Camus' final example of the absurd man, has a rather simplistic existence: to conquer those weaker individuals and subjugate them through conquest. It is through the conqueror's portrayal as liberator that lures the oppressed minority into a false sense of security and hope prior to the objectification and subservience of the conquered. The conquistador imposes his will upon the weaker minority; and it is through this "show of power" that absurdly (dis)enables one from the other. The conqueror uses the minority as a means to an end. This demonstration of dominance is one that marginalizes the minority, thereby subjugating them, not as individuals but, as entities that have lost heir individuality.

Even though it *may* appear that Camus' *Myth* is superficial and incomplete (for it lacks in-depth analysis), it does allow, and becomes, a kind of prelude to the second installment in the Absurd Cycle: *The Rebel*. By the time that Camus approaches *The Rebel*, he "already had a plan in mind for a new trilogy of books on revolt...."[59] If this was not enough to substantiate his desire to move from the Absurd as a philosophy (or a possible address to the Existentialists), Camus chooses to focus on the political principles that would appear in *The Rebel*:

> ...only by understanding the absurd as an experience of ambivalence, as a kind of 'intellectual malady' with dangerous consequences and about which we must be vigilant, will we be able to comprehend the moral consequences of the absurd.[60]

Between Camus "the individual" and Camus "the thinker", there is a paradigm-shift in becoming more politically aware. It is in this awareness that the Absurd Man evolves into the rebel.

Fifteen years after its initial publication, Camus explains his ideological reasoning between *The Myth* and *The Rebel*:

> For me, "*The Myth of Sisyphus*" marks the beginning of an idea which I was to pursue in The Rebel. It attempts to resolve the problem of suicide, as The Rebel attempts to resolve that of murder.... [...] In all the books I have written since, I have attempted to pursue this direction.[61]

The rebel *cannot* be absurd because absurdity precludes a kind of nihilistic existence. Even the rebel who commits suicide, for example, is not entirely absurd. Yes, according to Camus, those who commit suicide have devalued their lives; yet, the suicide bomber has found purpose and meaning in the act of suicide (bombing) even if it is a means to an end.

---

[59] Hawes, 64

[60] Bowker, 226

[61] Camus, *MS*, v

Dostoevsky's characters are among the most philosophically complex in all of literature. In fact Kirilov, from *The Possessed*, is metaphysically absurd through the constant ebbing and flowing of God's creation and destruction. While his suicide is "not a question of revenge, but of revolt"[62] it can be seen as a two-fold revolt: on the one hand, there is a metaphysical revolt against God or any other kind of Supreme Being; and on the other hand, there is a revolt for or against humanity.

Kirilov's metaphysical revolt is, as stated above, a revolt against God or another Supreme Being where to replace God is to kill God. "In order to fully rebel against the absurdity of human life, one must accept that neither history itself nor the Christian Church will provide any assistance in the midst of a world of "evil and death.""[63] However, in order to kill God, Kirilov must commit suicide - which denies the idea that God dominates all - because it places Kirilov in the position of acting as his own "god" - i.e. director of his own destiny. As Camus points out, this logic is flawed and fatalistic because "If God does not exist, Kirilov is God. If God does not exist, Kirilov must kill himself to become God."[64]

The humanitarian revolt is one where Kirilov chooses, or rather deludes himself into thinking that his suicide is achieved out of love for humanity[65], thereby constructing himself into a kind of "sacrificial lamb" where he is not victimized but "crucified." Thus it is the noble and ultimate sacrifice of his life, for that higher cause, that confers both value and meaning onto an otherwise meaningless existence. Again, Human rebellion ends in metaphysical revolution...When the throne of God is overturned, the rebel realizes that it is now his own responsibility to create the justice, order, and unity that he sought in vain within his condition, and in this way to justify the fall of God. Then begins the desperate effort create, at the price of crime and murder if necessary, the dominion of man.[66]

---

[62] Camus, *MS*, 106

[63] Sleasman, 77.

[64] Camus, *MS*,106

[65] Ibid, 108

[66] Bowker, 234

The Rebel continues where The Myth of Sisyphus leaves off. For example, in the Introduction to The Rebel, Camus states that "There are crimes passion and crimes of logic."[67] And while Camus' first literary and loosely philosophical work The Stranger addresses the lack of passion and logic within its protagonist, Meursault, there is recognition, on Camus' part, of Kirilov being both passionate and logical in his quest and decision to rebel against society. Awareness of passion and logic lead to the discovery of meaning; and it is meaning, in turn, that negates the Absurd, and provides a basis for the rebel in The Rebel. According to Camus scholar Matthew Bowker:

> In The Rebel, Camus no longer argues simply that the awareness of absurdity leads to the moral conclusion of rebellion, as he did in The Myth of Sisyphus. He does claim that absurd awareness leads to absurd rebellion, but he also defends a corollary proposition: that rebellion leads to an awareness, a fuller awareness of the absurd.[68]

Yet, if one examines the evolution of the Absurd from Camus' earlier ideas in The Myth, then one can see that awareness of the Absurd leads to the "dramatic" end of suicide. This proves to be the opposite in The Rebel because meaning has been found in the means to the end; this negates the nihilistic tendencies of the Absurd through the awareness. For the rebel, then, one must choose to live; and by choosing to live, one becomes aware, where awareness negates the Absurd.

For the rebel, awareness is also an affirmation of life. Thus, this identity gives the rebel his first sense/degree of self-worth. Silence should not be taken as a sign of apathy or of indifference. On the contrary, it should be seen as a mode of reflection.

Readers begin to see the metamorphosis of Sisyphus into the Rebel through his degrees of self-worth: for example, one's awareness leads to recognition (or cognition) of his self-worth, which would lend itself to his purpose — that is, his belief that rebellion is necessary and justified;

---

[67] Camus, The Rebel 3

[68] Bowker, 226.

obviously, this would constitute a form of anti-nihilism. From the rebel's belief in justification, one is able to choose between: murder, suicide or pacifism? While both murder and suicide constitute an active role in rebellion, pacifism would be seen as more passive. Even though the goals of both types of rebels justify the means and the ends, the pacifist could be seen as active in his own right through a positive, yet submissive role where he is acting for positive change through non-violent means. This can lead to action, which is a form of rebellion; and finally, during rebellion the rebel identifies himself with others - both active individuals and the repressed and oppressed individuals that he is trying to liberate. These two final stages of the rebel's metamorphoric existence lead to what Camus refers to as "metaphysical rebellion."

Metaphysical rebellion is a protest against conditions *and* creation.[69] The protest is enacted out of frustration towards the universe for and because of the conditions and environment of the rebel. The "ethical" element contained within the protest is where the rebel protests (out of) the value of (in which) he finds himself.[70] While in *The Myth*, the contemplation of suicide might be seen as a blasphemy of the self (or of God, if one is theistic), rebellion, as an act, according to Camus, is blasphemous towards or against society. Both suicide and rebellion constitute a conscious disagreement from and against a higher, governing authority—hence, the blasphemy.

The rebel posits himself against an empowering and objectifying existing power which is what he rebels against. It is his rebellion that affirms his existence as a self and as an entity—i.e. making him a rebel. However, it is the actual action of rebellion that identifies his sense of self because he is, after all, that which defines him. His existence as a rebel precedes his essence as such. One must exist prior to the essence of definition. The slave is still a slave until he takes action and rebels, not just choosing to rebel.

Slaves, who can be seen as a prototypical rebel, are already objectified and are forced into either: their continued submission or their

---

[69] Camus, *The Rebel,*23

[70] Ibid, 23

rebellion. Their existence is an either/or. Again, according to Bowker, "Camus' metaphysical rebel, who is also a slave, appears to rebel on the grounds of unity ... in the context of absurd ambivalence."[71]

Defined as such, the slave is objectified as a "thing-in-itself"; yet, he can be seen as a being-for-others (and not in the Sartrean sense) as a thing for others. Thus, there are essentially two types of slaves: those who choose not to rebel and continue their submission, perhaps because of their inability to revolt, or perhaps because of their complacency with their existence. The other type of rebel is the one who chooses to break the shackles of oppression and rebel. The slave is not going to be defined by his oppressors or the oppressors' objectification but, rather, he will create his own definition through his actions.

In fact, the most supreme of the former slaves - turned rebel - is Satan, who, as Camus states, "...rises against his Creator because the latter employed force to subjugate him."[72] One could argue that Satan has not other choice but to rebel against God's suppression, and that it is necessary for Satan's continued existence. And while Satan's rebellion is fatalistic (after all, Satan knows that his rebellion against God is doomed to failure), he must go through with the rebellion in order to affirm and assert his existence as a rebel both to himself and to God. Thus, this leads to Satan's own sense of self-justification of his actions, and makes Satan out to be a Judeo-Christian Sisyphus.

Like Satan's fatalistic decision to rebel humans are, understandably, compelled, by nature, to rebel against oppressive forces. When the rebel chooses to rebel, he chooses to reject the salvation of God because he takes his life and actions into own hands. He stands up against the tyranny that restrains his freedom and denies any suppressive power over him. For the rebel, there is only one entity that can save him - and that is himself. Like Kirilov, once the rebel decides to rebel, he negates God's existence in order to become God in the name of morality. And Satan is no exception.

---

[71] Bowker, 227

[72] Camus, *The Rebel*, 48

When the rebel, including Satan, chooses to rebel, he chooses to reject any type or hope of salvation from God. This is because through the rejection of salvation, the rebel has negated the need for God's existence by taking his life and actions into his own hands.[73] Once the rebel has negated and rejected God's salvation, he is ready to affirm his own existence. This is what Nietzsche was trying to accomplish, among other ideas, when he affirmed that "God is dead."

Camus' synthesis of Nietzsche's aphorism and its relationship with metaphysical rebellion is worthy of noting:

> If nihilism is the inability to believe, then its most serious symptom is not found in atheism, but in the inability to believe in what is, to see what is happening, and to live life as it is offered. This infirmity is at the root of all idealism.[74]

Nietzsche's (in)famous claim that God is dead has been misconstrued by generations of individuals since its conception in the 1880s, and while I will not digress into the vortex of debate is to Nietzsche's apparent and significant atheism, I claim that the moment and intention of Nietzsche's assertion is one that he maintains as the launching point of rebellion.

Religious connotations aside, if the "real" or metaphorical God is dead, indeed, then as Kirilov points out: everything is permitted. The rebel, not having an authority to rebel against, must assume the role of God and in doing must rebel against himself. According to Camus, who interprets Nietzsche, rebellion begins with the death of God. While rebellion against God is a rebellion against the injustice and hypocrisy of Christianity (as Nietzsche originally intended), it was not Nietzsche who "killed" God. It was his contemporaries—mainly the Romantics, who sought refuge in the self and away from a Supreme Being. Nietzsche, however, turned out to be society's convenient scapegoat.

---

[73] Ibid, 55

[74] Ibid, 67

Again, coming to Nietzsche's aid is Camus who states that according to Nietzsche Christ's message that salvation will be for those of good deeds, not faith.[75] Of course, this negates the purpose of faith that has been placed as an emphasis, on individuals, by the church, because to not believe entirely is an act of rebellion, and Christianity believes in fighting against rebellion in order to give the former its purpose and a sense of direction.[76] Camus believes that this is a kind of solipsistic nihilism as it imposes an imaginary meaning on life which prevents the discovery of real meaning; it clouds judgment.

For Camus, it is here with the denial of God in the name of morality that is cause for the idiom "everything is permitted", which is seen as the beginning of nihilism. Yet, the question must be asked, "How does the rebel reconcile nihilism with his ideals?" Well, the rebel will either rebel out of despondency - which is a moderate form of nihilism, or he will choose to rebel against the oppressive existence giving himself a purpose that indicatively nullifies nihilism. Either way, the mere action of rebellion is one in which is cause for the rebel to find meaning, purpose and the annulment of nihilism. "A nihilist is not one who believes in nothing, but one who does not believe in what exists."[77]

The purpose of the rebel is one where:

> The free mind will destroy... values and denounce the illusions on which they were built, the bargaining that they imply and the crime they commit in preventing the lucid intelligence from accomplishing its mission: to transform passive nihilism into active nihilism.[78]

---

[75] Ibid, 68.

[76] Ibid, 69.

[77] Ibid, 69.

[78] Ibid, 70.

For the rebel, "The joy of self-realization is the joy of annihilation. But only the individual is annihilated. The movement of rebellion, by which man demanded his own existence, disappears in the individual's absolute submission to the inevitable. Amor fati replaces what was an odium fati."[79] (To speak of love replaces what was to speak of hate.)

---

[79] Ibid, 70.

Bibliography

Bowker, Matthew. "Meursault and Moral Freedom: The Stranger's Unique Challenge to an Enlightenment Ideal." *The Journal of the Albert Camus Society* (2009): 22-45. Print.

Bronner, Stephen Eric. *Albert Camus: The Thinker, The Artist, The Man.* Canada: Watts, 1996. Print.

Camus, Albert. *The Myth of Sisyphus.* Trans. Justin O'Brien. New York: Vintage, 1955. Print.

- - -. *The Rebel.* Trans. Anthony Bower. New York: Vintage, 1956. Print.

Dostoevsky, Fyodor. *Notes From Underground.* Trans. Michael R. Katz. New York: Norton, 2001. Print.

Hawes, Elizabeth. *Camus, A Romance.* New York: Grove Press, 2009. Print.

Nietzsche, Friedrich. *The Will to Power.* Trans. Walter Kaufmann. New York: Vintage, 1967. Print.

Sleasman, Brent. "The Philosophy of Communication as the Absurd: Albert Camus and the Ethics of Everyday." *The Journal of the Albert Camus Society* (2009): 45-71. Print.

Solidarity of the Absurd – the Invisible Philosopher in the Writing of Albert Camus

By Svenja Schrahé

The literary works of this writer ... philosopher ... this is exactly where the problem starts. How do you call someone who did not want to be called a philosopher, at least not one of a specific kind? Does this imply one can only belong to one category at a time? If so, it must yet be possible to switch categories like 'philosopher' or 'litterateur' after some decades. On the other hand, is this person a writer just because words are put onto paper? Albert Camus himself rejected the idea of being judged as an existential philosopher, his writing should be regarded as a whole – literature in pure. Existentialism like the rest of philosophical movements stands in a long tradition, each with its own history and praised thinkers. Does it make Camus even more of a philosopher to reject this tradition loaded label or does it make him more of a writer?

The difference between the two is bigger than just a rearrangement of words. A literary philosopher is an actual thinker that compiles his work in a literary genre widely or more easily understood by his audience. A philosophy needs to be shared so that it does not remain a construct within the area of the brain. When it is brought to paper it automatically enters the dimension of a literary level. However, the genre for this kind of literature lives in a purely free area because its origin lies in philosophy. A thought originated and labelled in the area of philosophy, i.e. existentialism, stoicism, solipsism etc., has no boundaries and no limits or restrictions as faced in the normal literary milieu. The finished text of a literary philosopher does therefore not fit in the judgement of a literary critic but needs to be examined under the circumstances of philosophy. Roland Barthes' idea of the death of the author might exclude Camus the same way he excluded him out of philosophy, but then only a very brief part of his work is left and this rest-literature feels forced. Consequently one asks: where is the invisible philosopher in Camus' work?

The book *Nausea* by Jean-Paul Sartre, a contemporary of Albert Camus, but also a friend until their breaking off in 1952, is naturally considered literature. Yet, the philosopher in it is much more present than in the work of Camus. The protagonist of Sartre's *Nausea* is a pure embodiment of his whole existential concept, facing the fact that there is no metaphysical higher power, no creature able to evoke the impression of a meaning or sense in life. Sartre's conclusion for his philosophy is then further reflected in his books: humankind is doomed to be free. The conclusion how Sartre got here is more interesting than the actual examination of life as doom or fate. But does this conclusion come from his mind or from the paper? The first impression is that Sartre's overall feeling is disgust; Camus' in contrast is absurdity.[i] This can be shown by comparing the occurrence of these two words in the works of both authors. When Sartre's protagonist of *Nausea*, Antoine Roquentin, states:

> "A feeling of immense disgust suddenly flowed over me and the pen fell from my fingers, spitting ink. What had happened? Had I got the Nausea?"[80]

Compared to Meursault in *The Outsider*:

> "From the depths of my future throughout the whole of this absurd life I'd been leading, I'd felt a vague breath drifting towards me across all the years that were still to come"[81]

The word 'philosopher' is often used in summaries and biographies because a certain intellectual standard swings with it. Yet it remains unknown what the word 'philosopher' offers to the reader, to the critic and most of all to the writer. Philosophy differs enormously from literature as it wants engagement in thinking while literature in its genres often exists for the pure pleasure of reading. A literary engagement is thus based on a much freer basis. Understanding is the key word that needs to be taken into account.

---

[80] Jean Paul Sartre, *Nausea,* transl. Robert Baldick (London: Penguin, 1965), p. vii.

[81] Albert Camus, *The Outsider,* transl. Joseph Lardeo (London: Penguin, 1982), p. 115.

Even today a lot of people tend to avoid philosophy on the bookshelves because it is supposed to be heavy and difficult literature. Regarding the sheer size of some philosophy books it sure has a point.

How can two fields that have so different aims be combined and appear to be one of the same kinds at times? The answer is simpler than the construct. It goes back to the struggle of critics what is more important: the text or the writer? The same question applies to philosophy and literature – the thought or the written word? A more general rule in society says that if one cannot put thoughts down into words, nobody will understand them. The answer is definitely uncertain as even the most worded thought can remain a mystery.

Another important feature of 'understanding' is the active thinking of the reader or critic along with the text. There is no need to compile a work when the audience cannot follow a single idea. Understanding philosophy is an art for itself just like there are hundreds of books and pamphlets written of how to understand poetry or literature in general. If there is no active engagement of what is written or thought then there would be no need to deal with it – not to question is the death of philosophy. Philosophy's motor is questioning and the basis for this is comprehension and finding new ways of looking at it. Literature knows about this questioning as well. All literary movements are basically a question of old worldviews, which is possibly a reason why terms like 'modernism' or 'post-modernism' are so vague. There is no fix explanation given. Whenever something is read or thought through with new generations there will be new ways to look at it and new definitions will be added. Philosophy is, however, more difficult to revise and expand because we believe that thoughts are free and freedom is a sacred value. The debate has to do with judgement and the belief that highly regarded former philosophers are untouchable: their statements are not to be challenged.

From a literary point of view there is a way out, namely when philosophy enters literature in terms of becoming a written piece of work. A word unlike a thought undergoes country or language specific rules, for example grammar and orthography. Further, words have a meaning, they are not blank sheets. In a way, words enable automatically an access for both the compiler, namely the philosopher transforming to become a writer, and the reader, who knows what the words mean. The reader is then able to look through these to the philosopher's ideas and gain a new meaning what words mean. This has less to do with double-meaning, but more with the adjusting to another genre – the one of literature. The transformation progress and not the final work is where philosophy and literature come as close as possible, the choice of words is crucial and important. A lot of words can be found for emotions, beautifully arranged and evoke these described feelings in the reader or the thinker. However, showing a rational thought and making this thought one of the audience's is a more difficult task. Thinking and writing enter the same circle and interchange their history as well as their features, i.e. grammar, history, meaning and genres. It is only a vicious circle when the writer fails to acknowledge the transformation and is fixed by standing firmly on the label of either 'literature' or 'philosophy'. If the combination of the two goes smoothly, the audience is presented a double-layered meaningful text; an image where two snakes biting each other's tail rather than a literary ride to hell. Jonathan Baron adds another argument by saying that "Good thinking requires a thorough search for possibilities—other things being equal."[82] Consequently, and at least in thinking, philosophy and literature are equal. Therefore, authorship and philosophy must be equal as well and hold the balance.

Going back a bit, the central connection (=understanding) between philosophy and literature is itself based on two pillars: reception and expectation. Reception or in general receiving a text is an important feature of philosophy as it makes it even more accessible. When it is put into words, hence a piece of literature, it enters an even wider audience. The kind of audience and intelligence is first of all not important in this part as the reception is purely constructed by the philosopher or writer and projected onto the reader. Expectation, on the other hand, is a certain attitude towards the text that arouses by reading the first few lines of it. Every reader starts his own judgement and interpretation during this action and concludes for himself what might happen next. If the expectation is acceptable or good, there is more projected on the characters in literature and the author in philosophy. Important is here as well the style of writing which means even the most foreign philosopher to literary genres cannot deny the fact that the choice of words has to follow rules. In the first instance, grammar and simplification of a subject seems to be central, because it opens itself to a wide readership. To be more precise, it is also the author's decision which

---

[82] Jonathan Baron, *Thinking and deciding, 4th ed.* (Cambridge: Cambridge University Press, 2008), p. 62.

audience he chooses. There is always the fear that any description in the text and the intended cut at the end of a chapter or page is disappointing. Not only the prospective reader, but also the philosopher as a writer is trying to find the exact words to explain his thinking.

What does this exactly look like and how does it work? Albert Camus cleverly avoided that problem with a conception which can be called the 'exposed restraint' and it describes the ability to demonstrate the thinking and feeling of a character through a monologue or an echoed monologue in a dialogue. An echoed monologue is quite often used in the writing of Camus. In his book *The Fall*, Jean-Baptiste Clamence constantly demonstrates it. Just like the whole philosophy of the absurd as shown in Sartre's *Nausea*, there is no need for another existence around as long as thoughts are demonstrated. At the very beginning of the book, Jean-Baptiste is talking with someone in the bar in the city of Amsterdam. Besides the description of a barkeeper with an incredible accent, there is no surrounding given – everything remains vague, everything remains plain and simple – shortly: a frame. Clamence is one figure inside this frame, basically giving a long monologue about the incidents in his life, however, the reader is able to read this thoughts and events because they are projected onto him. In a way, the reader becomes part of the frame and picture at the same time. Without a framework, Clamence would completely fall out of his thoughts – a method earlier used as the stream of consciousness and popular for its endless precision.

Connecting it with reception and expectation, *The Fall* enables a good ground to see how these concepts interact as representations of philosophy and literature. Both fields are again joined by saying that some metaphors or expressions used in a text can be taken "literally". It means that words act on two levels, the literary one and the one we give them. The concept is already known as connotation and denotation in language, but it could also be transformed by saying: a word acts on two levels – namely the philosophic and the literary one. The first level contains the earlier mentioned expectations on a lower stage, combining the thoughts and philosophy of an author as well as the reader. The second level also represents on a lower stage reception and how appropriate the reader and author dealt with a text. Literature is the result, philosophy the progress, but as soon as literature is dealt with, it undergoes further progresses (=philosophy) and becomes a result (=literature) again when the thinking has ended. Since thinking never really ends, philosophy and literature act again like two snakes biting each other in the tails. The whole levelling can be seen as a staircase in a surreal painting, where the snakes go up and down. One book on this staircase is, as mentioned, *The Fall*.

The fall described in the book is not only the literal, e.g. the woman on the bridge. It is rather the fall of judgment, the Fall of Man. It seems like Clamence ate the apple, gained too much knowledge and is still falling out of heaven, but this time his self-created, hypocrite heaven. Whenever he encounters another person, his eloquence can cover up most of his flaws, but when it comes to action and reaction, Clamence is stiff and stuck in himself. In a way, he cannot let himself fall far enough to actually do something and be human. His position is to judge in advance and stay in secret distance to life. Only in the end, Clamence realizes that if he wants to move on, he needs to make a final judgment on himself. Society lets him go away with every sin and non-action he did – he is a lawyer, so he got the backstage pass to the little holes in life. It is what we call unfair, that some people are able to get away with everything, but in the end, their punishment is themselves. Sartre's saying, that real hell is in ourselves, becomes painfully true in the life that Clamence shows us. The last gesture is to provoke someone to judge him that is why he owns a part of the Ghent Altarpiece, The Just Judges, reflecting ironically what he is desperately longing for: a just judge. The society around him and even the reader is not a reliable just judge since they just take in the information and let go, being (like Clamence) way too concerned with their own lives.

Every positive attribute (expectation) in the beginning is turned around into a negative one, he slowly announces the reader his vanity, his excessive way of life but also his inability to connect with others (reception). It is at this time that Clamence cannot hamper the suicide of a young girl, because it would mean to get his own life at risk. Clamence is a hypocrite who is aware of his flaws, someone so deeply stuck in his own crisis that his way of dealing is to ignore and leave it. A blind person cannot watch the bowing gesture, only outsiders can. The whole monologue appears to be a confession, a confession of how we all make judgments and how wrong judgments can haunt our lives. The judging starts in the beginning with the Dutch bartender, whose accent he is teasing, then further the Dutch people, his home – the French and also Parisians, the woman on the bridge, the motorcyclist he encounters and so forth.

What makes the book *The Fall* so special is the whole communication, which is based on a single person. It is a postmodern one-way, only one direction is given but no higher pattern where it is going. The answers received in the book are spoken out loud by Clamence, without his narcissistic attitude to repeat the spoken word the reader is given nothing but a projection. In a way, it is the book next to Camus' *The Stranger* where the main character is mute, his only speech resembles an echo of the talking around him. It does not answer how reliable Clamence is as a narrator. An example gives Clamence changing attitude towards speaking:

> "But I'm not really feeling myself this evening, either. I'm even having trouble forming a sentence. I get the feeling that I'm not speaking fluently and I'm expressing myself less well."[83]

And by the end of the story Clamence admits himself

> "I knew we belonged to the same breed. Aren't we all the same, continually talking, addressing non one, constantly raising the same questions, even though we know the answers before we start?"[84]

It questions also the professions of people, how much they can tell us about lives and eventually Camus lets us take look into the mirror: we are all like Clamence, busy with ourselves, taking the distance and making assumptions in advance. It is what makes us human, but sometimes there is this lesson to learn to let go, just *fall*, in order not to end like the Jean-Baptiste.

Despite philosophy and literature in this work falling into each other and reflecting the level imagery mentioned, the idea of projection should be examined in more detail. The first concepts of the projection theory that actually considered the human nature and thus humanity as a valuable aim to achieve go back to question religion. It needs to be said that religion is not questioned throughout the following lines. Speaking in terms of Camus, it is

---

[83] Albert Camus, *The Fall,* transl. Robin Buss (London: Penguin, 2006), p. 27.

[84] Camus, *The Fall*, p. 92.

as absurd as the rest of all construction, but necessary to keep humans alive if we acknowledge the fact of absurdity in it.

German philosopher Ludwig Feuerbach was the first one who actually transformed the idea of projection from supernatural to natural basics. In his works, he mainly argues that religion as a whole in a concept is the projection of human values and human needs onto something divine. Despite the criticism of religious defenders arguing about the need of humanity to project and create something divine, the basic idea can be found in the works of Camus as well. Feuerbach's basic is the nature, the nature of man, the nature of desire and the man in a world of unity. Since his idea should be connected to the one of Camus quite easily, the word solidarity should appear where unity was set. Feuerbach argued that nature got more and more idealised and an object was born, where wishes appeared instead of action and reality. A bit of a dream world as it resembled reality and was soon unattainable or believed to be unattainable. Through the creation of a divine being, which is called God or Divine Spirit, man puts himself in chains and completely disconnects from reality and nature. Therefore, nature is the original, god would be the copy. In other words, human nature, namely ourselves, is the original in the works of Camus. The copy is what we call life and what needs to be filled with certain achievements – otherwise it is not a life worth living. Where Feuerbach puts his projection theory, Camus describes the clash with absurd thinking. The aspect of acceptance connects both thinkers and writers - Feuerbach suggests that humankind needs to accept the self and through this create a humanistic philosophy, a conception that cares about the ordinary man and overcomes the strict and dividing bounds of religious dogmas. It may therefore be materialistic, but it is at least graspable and there in the present life, not the afterlife. Thomas Wartenberg sums up Feuerbach's expectation by saying that "Feuerbach thought that human beings could come to realize their own divinity, thus creating a world in which the human race could fully realize its potential as a species."[85]

Camus incorporates this humanity in his thinking through acceptance of the absurd. By doing so, humankind is automatically connected with one

---

[85] Ludwig Feuerbach, *Principles of the philosophy of the future*, transl. Manfred H. Vogel; Introduction Thomas E. Wartenberg (Indianapolis, Ind.: Hackett Pub. Co., 1986), p viii.

another (solidarity) and therefore overcomes the schizophrenic credo of life: meaning and senselessness.

The method used by Camus as described in *The Fall* resembles not only the projection but also an echo. The reader is inside the head of the character or author. According to the explained projection theory the reception and expectation would make him understand and become more involved with the text. Consequently, the echo is a part of the result when the projection theory worked its whole way down the staircase. It is one of the main keys that are needed to unlock the meaning. Besides several approaches to text that question whether to divide the author from his text or not, the echo stands outside this question as it is truly more philosophic in its approach. The echo unlocks the intended meaning. First of all because it displays the whole process of writing done by the philosopher or author and puts them inside the head of the reader. However, at the same time it unlocks the unintended meaning, where the reader is encouraged to think about what is read. Thinking is an issue that leads back to the very nature and so to say fuel of philosophy. The chain reaction is that a questioning follows of what was read and questioning requires understanding, so in the end the circle is closed. Three items interchange generally in this circle, the text, the author and the reader. All of them can appear in all their possible mathematical hierarchies yet the result is that their engagement leads back to *question-understanding-projection-echo-question*... and so forth.

In his book *The Stranger* Camus shows this interchanging connection where he himself is the missing connection between the reader and Meursault as the main character. Furthermore, he represents a trait of Meursault's character, the inability to speak for himself, and thus enables the reader a new realm normally unattainable. He is the voice we miss when we talk to people or even sit next to them to remain silent together. Charisma and voice have always been vital and are still motives in each book where the author and the characters hit the boundary. While reading, there is a cinema in our head and we long for hearing the voices and continue to turn the page. Interestingly, the inner cinema is one of the reasons why people are disappointed when the movie version is much worse than the book – their build up expectation did not correlate with the projection of the director. The reader encounters Meursault, just like Jean-Baptiste in *The Fall*, in his daily life, here at the funeral of his mother. Seeing how he does not cry, how he seems to be cold towards emotions and mute among other people. The situation reflects the philosophic idea of the absurd, but is in fact lying beneath the actual story.

"The caretaker turned the light-switch and I was blinded by the sudden blaze of light. He asked me if I wanted to go to the canteen to have some dinner. But I wasn't hungry. He then offered to bring me a cup of white coffee. I'm very fond of white coffee, so I accepted and he came back a few minutes later with a tray. I drank. I then wanted a cigarette. But I hesitated because I didn't know if I could smoke in front of mother. I thought it over, it really didn't matter. I offered the caretaker a cigarette and we smoked."[86]

Despite this indifference-philosophy, the actual narrator or what can be perceived through the echo as a narrator, is clearly unreliable. The reader never really knows what is going on. The chosen passage contains a time gap: when the caretaker, according to Meursault, leaves for some minutes, he is naturally alone with his mother. Yet, the reader has no idea what happened in these minuets and apparently Meursault himself does not record that either. Time is not a matter of organising a life in this book but just an event that ticks in the background. The picture as a whole remains one-dimensional. Through this literary style, it challenges the reader more than it does in the first instance with its philosophy. Again, every sentence is nearly indirect speech and even the active ones appear indirect since we are not able to hear them. Camus is the echo that keeps the whole method rolling, but without him the reader would try to approach a hermetic text. Hermeticism does not only work in exile or war poetry during the second half of the 20th century, but also in the novel or a philosophic text. In fact, every text contains a specific amount of Hermeticism that needs to be unlocked. The idea is to make the text accessible to only a specific audience. Now, it would stand in contrast to the above mentioned idea to make a text understandable for everyone. It sort of does because the philosopher or writer needs to be aware in the first place how closed or open his work should be.

The philosopher or writer decides and construct by mostly choosing metaphors and allusions, figures in writing that follow a clear logic and can be deciphered by the reader. In general, these devices can be collected for the following as symbols. Symbols, unlike words, resemble philosophy. They appear in a surrounding that does not follow grammar or style, it is the mind

---

[86] Camus, *The Outsider*, p. 14.

again where it is born. Put to paper, a symbol has a specific structure (just like philosophy) but is more variable than the word as even a fast drawn symbol shows the same unlike a word that lacks some letters. Hence, a style of hermetic writing has its limit, is literature with its chains. However, if the symbols are taken into account, this literature enters philosophy again and becomes unlimited in their minds. It forces the writer or philosopher to be creative in his words and convincing in his argument. In the works of Camus, the constant mesmerizing of existence through the absurd makes the reader automatically a part of the world as shown in the text, even if it is not realised. Existence is overall connecting and cannot be denied until death and even then the body still exists as in terms of being present and being real. In the end, it is not adjusting to the audience that centralises in his work, is the adjusting to the meaning. Meaning goes back to symbols and words and it also discusses the very basics of philosophy, namely if a word can build the basis for a theory and furthermore for a philosophy. It also queries if the word ends up enabling the connection to a literary genre. Absurdity or the absurd, the senselessness and negation of every value in life as unimportant and ridiculous, appears as an attitude that comes with the philosophy of existentialism. Eventually, the appearance of a word in a literary text can hint towards a certain attitude of philosophy but is by itself not philosophy. There is a high chance of overvaluing the word on its philosophical level (because the author is marked as one) and disregarding the literal level.

Camus' Essay *The Myth of Sisyphus* is an example of how symbols and words interact and enables a combination of philosophy and literature. The myth of the Sisyphus itself was preserved orally before it became known on paper; therefore, the decisive power is literature. The action of this man rolling up a stone, watching it roll down again and the turning to the person to lift it up once again becomes symbolic because its meaning is more important than the actual story behind Sisyphus. The question of punishment is not part of Camus' philosophy, it is generally assumed to be known and accepted. The stone in action becomes a representation of the absurd in Camus' philosophy. Put to paper it is also a written story about the character of Sisyphus which reminds us of Meursault and that Camus is the missing link between the character and the reader, echoing the punishment and the reader's expectation. Morality, ethics, philosophy, literature, all great social sciences are big words throughout the work of Albert Camus and basically every other writer in history. Their important connection is made up within the mind as the central train station from where each train departs. Philosophy as literature takes the crossroads not only through history but also through words and touches many other sciences, for example the importance of language and how the choice of words affects the style of writing. *The Fall* and *The Stranger* by Camus know about this power and they combined it perfectly just as philosophy embraces the tradition of literature and vice versa. Imagining a frame with an ever changing picture, it is not clear what field of science is inside or outside the frame or picture. Even though in a philosophic tradition, it is assumed that Camus himself did not think that far about the shape of his own philosophy as he states for himself in the *Myth of Sisyphus* that there is only one problem in philosophy, which is suicide and every other question comes after that. Camus simplifies the process of expectation for the reader as he cuts out a universal hierarchy of philosophy and focuses on one central aspect.

> "Judging whether life is or is not worth living amounts to answering the fundamental question of philosophy. All the rest – whether or not the world has three dimensions, whether the mind has nine or twelve categories – comes afterwards. These are games; one must first answer. ... These are facts the heart can feel; yet they call for careful study before they become clear to the intellect."[87]

The reference to suicide is not the simple tick on a list to cover the basics of human life and then continue, it is the touchstone of humanity – the question of what makes a person human and what drives him in his life. For Camus it is the ability to exist, the inner conflict to seek the ultimate meaning in life and the lack of fulfilment. It is also notably where philosophy enters literature and where the literature of Camus shakes hands with the ideas of Sartre.

The suggested action in the *Myth of Sisyphus* is the revolt and rebellion against the absurd as the road to real happiness, leaves the range of philosophy and literature and becomes a social, maybe even world-wide concern. By saying yes to a senseless life, approaching a way to happiness and embracing loneliness with a smile, people will join each other as a problem shared is one less to carry. This is not a remembrance of a Hippie gathering, but more a rational questioning of one's own life and the honesty to admit what is senseless. It truly is the solidarity of the absurd, but also freed from the chains of philosophy. Chains, because philosophy still has a dusty image, no matter how clever the cover is changed, it still remains an activity

---

[87] Albert Camus, *The Myth of Sisyphus,* transl. Justin O'Brien (London: Penguin, 2000), p. 11

in the brain, like a hamster wheel turning around. Sometimes it even is the scary vision of losing oneself in thoughts and break away from reality even though a feeling of what is real was the aim. These thoughts in the turning wheel become literature as soon as they enter the paper and actually appear in words arranged by grammar, so that they can be shared by a group; further in translation, they can shared by a whole nation and so forth. Yet, the ability to say yes to rebellion and live by another credo, namely the one of senselessness being a minor problem to this world, seems to be so easy that it leaves to the thinking processes of philosophy and the rules of literature. This step marks the transition when Camus' invisible philosophy steps out of the labelling shadow and becomes clear to the reader or critic. The rebellion of Camus does not care about rules, they are as absurd as the rest of us, though it does not support anarchy or chaos – the idea is guided and ruled by essential communal ideas: happiness and solidarity. They are also essentially invisible as Camus himself did not specify it or go into further detail. This can be regarded as a general superiority of philosophy, which also needs a clarification. Superiority does not mean the arrogance or actual better-than-attitude. It refers to the idea that essential features of humanity like happiness are so fundamental and present to us that there is no need to bother with questions of how many dimensions they have in relation to the universe. Robert A. Segal comments on Camus' usage of the myth, the philosophy and the humanity by commenting "Sisyphus was to be pitied. For Camus, he is to be admired. ... His is the only kind of heroism that a meaningless, because godless world allows. Camus uses the myth of Sisyphus to dramatize the human condition."[88]

Referring back to the 'needing' part of the construct, in combination with philosophy it shows that there has been and always will be a need for philosophy. Humankind will always think. The question is just how deep it will go down the staircase of thoughts, projection and expectation. For Camus, thinking is a matter of fact, and even the most absurd thought need to be embraced and accepted as we therefore accept our humanity, our flaws and mortality. This stands in clear contrast to previous philosophers like René Descartes whose discourse pre-created the way of totality, unity and disunity. Albert Camus' unity is reflected in the aspect of solidarity. Because of his statement that the real philosophical problems occur after suicide, which is as

---

[88] Robert A. Segal, *Myth: a very short introduction* (Oxford: Oxford University Press, 2004), p. 44.

elaborated the problem of existence, Camus does not appear to be a real philosopher that can be easily put into a form.

Anthropology as derived from the comparison between Feuerbach and Camus is another turning point, because it is where philosophy and literature unite perfectly and leave their snake state of being. In the works of Camus, anthropology is the essential feature that stands behind his parole to accept absurdity and revolt against it, become human and moreover one with yourself again. Our modern era reduced this principle to 'Accept and love yourself, only then others will love you'. For Camus, this chain reaction is of no importance, as the absurd moment and its revolution makes humankind equal and levels them down to their real selves: their existence. It may seem very unimportant for past philosophers who were concerned with the split of the body and the mind and how complicated our senses work against our drives, yet, the very fact that we exist as human beings is often taken for granted. French philosopher René Descartes, some centuries before Camus and often called the godfather of thinking, takes the point of existence into his philosophy and thinking. As a result, saying that both are alike or Camus being in tradition of Descartes is way too simplified and only partly correct when regarding philosophy and literature. Bringing the two fields together in the works of Albert Camus, it could be easily said that the credo of René Descartes 'I think, therefore I am' should be rewritten as 'I rebel, therefore I am'. This is only one part of the truth. The tendency to apply philosophic credos or statements to works because they sound right or very witty is often just the easy way out. Camus deals with rebellion, because he accepts absurdity while Descartes accepts his existence because he is thinking. The difference is obvious as Camus does not question the absurdity and the thinking behind it. The acceptance is of much more importance than the constant nagging on reality, hence the advice that suicide is the most important task to claim. Admittedly, suicide is a form of existence namely, as acknowledged by Camus, the question whether life is worth living or not. Tal Sessler sets this rebellion in accordance with a path for redemption. In a world without God and without rules, rebellion becomes a philosophy as Sessler explains that "reconciling oneself to the non-redemptive structure of the world in a post-theological epoch is paradoxically the sole path Camus envisages to achieving a sober 'redemption' from the chronic need to achieve totality and metaphysical unity."[89]

Imagine Camus and Descartes standing on the top of a roof, both thinking about suicide. Camus would be the one to conclude that it is senseless because the option of doing it is as absurd and conflicting as life itself. There is no solution even if life ends, it is just the ultimate end but not the fulfilment to a sense of life, therefore accepting this fact and stepping away from the edge to jump. In contrast, Descartes would not jump either but neither take a step backwards, because in his construct, his existence needs to be proven first to make sure that he is the one who wants to jump off the roof and not another person where there may no need to bother. By making sure he is the one losing his life, he would probably jump because his separation of the body and the mind would not harm his immortal soul. Leaving this comic behind, it is clear that by his writing Camus clearly stands out from the literary crowd as the invisible philosopher. An explanation why Camus would not jump can be found on the internet in an interview, where he defended himself against being called an 'absurdist'. Camus explains to the interviewer: "I was practicing methodical doubt. I was trying to make a "tabula rasa," on the basis of which it would then be possible to construct something. If we assume that nothing has any meaning, then we must conclude that the world is absurd. But does nothing have any meaning? I have never believed we could remain at this point."[90] Camus is too literary to be a philosopher in the classic sense yet inherits the tradition of questioning and rethinking. In contrast, his writing is often too philosophic to be pure literature.

The label of a philosopher is often used by literary critics to at least judge and define the works of an author. Criticism always has to start somewhere and it works best when there are certain points or terms within the history of philosophy or literature where the critic reader or thinker can start. The danger clearly lies in the need to overly criticise a work by the two main labels: philosophy or literature. Since philosophy still enjoys the privilege of

[89] Tal Sessler, *Levinas and Camus: humanism for the twenty-first century* (London: Continuum, 2008), p. 60.

[90] The Albert Camus Society of the UK, "Albert Camus and Existentialism," n.d., <http://www.camus-society.com/albert-camus-existentialism.html> (14 March 2010).

fools by being mainly in the mind and not on paper, literature tends to be largely judged on style, words, semantics rather than ideas. The term itself, namely philosophy as literature is questionable as the roles of both studies are not entirely clear. It can be assumed that through the variety of Camus' works there are more philosophers that could be described as philosophical writers instead of literary philosophers. The invisibility is not a disguise. There is no necessity to hide philosophy in literary works because they are expressed with them and through them. It is the old discussion of how to form ideas and how to make them visible. Visibility like its negation, invisibility, is not covered in words and can be printed. It is more concerned with how much is revealed. Every author has some ideas that work over and over again in a text, throughout history this is called philosophy; in this essay, it was called echo as this is more precise and describes directly the relationship of the author to his environment. Just as in science, there is an action in the text that is clear by the first reading. However, if the reader or thinker has the key to produce another action like re-reading, the invisible philosophy is revealed. This strategy contains the will to understand and to echo the parts of projection as they are part of the thinking.

This is the whole point that makes Albert Camus an outstanding modern writer. His strategy to make his invisible philosophy clear is covered in his statement of solidarity. We as readers and thinkers are solidary with the author, text or ideas, it does not really matter which part as one links back with the other. The invisibility of philosophy in literature is especially covering criticism. A protection shield that does not hasten judgement but takes time to value the effort of a philosopher challenging literature or a writer challenging the field of philosophy. But how much of a philosopher is Camus in reality? Quoting Tal Sessler once more here it states that "Camus establishes himself as the philosopher of the absurd. The 'death of God' constitutes the birth of the absurd."[91] These are the two key factors: the self-establishing of an author and the birth of a subtle philosophy. Both studies need to be understood in their interchanging relation, because the interpretation and conclusions of a text are much more fruitful than judging authorship and philosophy as separate sciences. This is, what it would do – denounce them to science, to simple action and reaction and even though some steps may appear to be scientific, it is just as Camus said that humans are driven by their absurd nature. Only this kind of acceptance makes us lose

---

[91] Sessler, p. 13.

the absurd chains to appreciate the value of life's creation – may it be philosophy or literature or both of them.

Bibliography

Baron, Jonathan. *Thinking and deciding, 4th ed*. Cambridge: Cambridge University Press, 2008.

Camus, Albert. *The Outsider*. Translated by Joseph Lardeo. London: Penguin, 1982.

Camus, Albert. *The Fall*. Translated by Robin Buss. London: Penguin, 2006.

Camus, Albert. *The Myth of Sisyphus*. Translated by Justin O'Brien. London: Penguin, 2000.

Feuerbach, Ludwig. *Principles of the philosophy of the future*. Translated by Manfred H.

Vogel; Introduction by Thomas E. Wartenberg. Indianapolis, Ind.: Hackett Pub. Co., 1986)

Sartre, Jean Paul. *Nausea*. Translated from the French by Robert Baldick. London: Penguin, 2000.

Segal, Robert A. *Myth: a very short introduction*. Oxford: Oxford University Press, 2004.

Sessler, Tal. *Levinas and Camus: humanism for the twenty-first century*. London: Continuum, 2008.

The Albert Camus Society of the UK, "Albert Camus and Existentialism," n.d., <http://www.camus-society.com/albert-camus-existentialism.html> (14 March 2010)

Father Paneloux, Alyosha Karamazov, and Deference to a God Who Allows the Suffering of Children

By Stephen Cranney

> *The creatures of Dostoevsky, we now know well, are neither strange nor absurd. They are like us, we have the same heart.*—Albert Camus, qtd. in Davison, 7

Dostoevsky's themes, characters, and issues are prevalently treated in Camus's own works. In particular, the character Ivan Karamazov from *The Brothers Karamazov* is extensively and explicitly analyzed in *The Rebel*. Secondary commentators have also thoroughly analyzed Dostoevsky's influence on Camus (for example, see Davison's *Camus: The Challenge of Dostoevsky*). However, much of this analysis has been directed towards Ivan, the representative of secularist intellectualism in Dostoevsky's *The Brothers Karamazov*. Much less attention has been paid by commentators to Ivan's younger brother Alyosha. I have only been able to identify one passage in one article that makes a brief mention of the connection between Alyosha and *the Plague*:

> Camus—who admired Dostoevsky as Dostoevsky admired Dickens—echoes and opposes the argument of *The Brothers Karamazov* when, in *The Plague*, he describes the death of the son of the city magistrate. In earlier fiction the actual dying of children is discreetly veiled or wholly omitted; here the physical process is recorded in agonizing, almost clinical detail. The effect of this suffering is devastating to both Dr. Rieux and Father Paneloux. Rieux's response is existential revolt: like Dostoevsky's Ivan, he cannot accept a "scheme of things in which children are put to torture." And Paneloux, who struggles to retain his faith, must finally argue that if God wills a child's suffering and death, he and other Christians must will it too. Thus Camus subverts the religious overtones associated with a child's death in *The Brothers*

Karamazov as well as in so many other nineteenth-century novels. We have moved into the twentieth century: the death of children that creates faith in Dostoevsky destroys it in Camus. (Hawkins viii)

While there is little or no material that explicitly focuses on the figure of Alyosha within the context of Camus, and while little explicit attention was paid to Alyosha by Camus himself in his commentaries on *The Brothers Karamazov,* I will argue that the figure of Alyosha is subtly and intertextually commented on through the person of Father Paneloux in *The Plague,* and that this character writes back into Dostoevsky's characters and themes.

In this paper I will first trace the correspondence between these two characters and establish their intertextual relationship through a discussion of four correspondence points between Camus's Father Paneloux and Dostoevsky's Alyosha: the recognition of the problematic theological questions raised by the suffering of children, the demand for a coherent mechanism for reconciling the suffering of children, the invocation of Christian symbolism in their attempt to provide such a justification, and the rejection of a form of afterlife utilitarianism as a means of justification. While I have not been able to find an explicit statement from Camus himself connecting these two characters, the abovementioned similarities, along with Camus's well-documented concern for the issues and characters of Dosteovsky, strongly suggest a literary relationship.

After establishing this relationship, I will examine the implications of Father Paneloux for Alyosha. Father Paneloux provides a detailed account of his thought processes and rationale involved in his decisions, while Alyosha provides some clues, but is vague enough to leave his own thoughts open to interpretation. Through Father Paneloux's record, we are allowed a glimpse an interpretation of Alyosha that, while granting legitimacy to some of his existential premises, ultimately attempts to discredit the final outcome of Dostoevsky's Christian existentialism. Specifically, I address three themes. The first is the identification of Alyosha's faith as a pragmatically-based one which, although it is hinted at in *Brothers Karamazov,* is not conclusive. This is related to the second point, which is that such a view naturally includes a degree of epistemological angst. This is more controversial, as Dostoevsky himself explicitly denies this at times.

However, his ambiguity on the issue allows for an alternative interpretation manifested in the person of Father Paneloux, thus questioning the validity of an honest, non-skeptical faith. Finally, the fate of Father Paneloux, diametrically opposite of that found in *Brothers Karamazov*, provides a commentary on the end result of a Dostoevskian existentialist faith.

Establishing the Intertextual Relationship

First, both characters recognize the problem of children's suffering as uniquely singular, categorically set apart from the traditional problem of suffering. Ivan Karamazov succinctly states that "I'm not talking about the suffering of grownups; they ate the apple and to hell with them, let the devil take them all, but these little ones!" (Dostoevsky 242) The Edenic metaphor indicates a degree of complicity on the part of the adults that is lacking in the children. Adults have fallen due to their own agency; they both receive and administer suffering, and consequently receive less empathy from Ivan, forcing him to "narrow [his] theme" (Dostoevsky 243). Children maintain a state of innocence that makes any suffering directed towards them absurd, putting into question the kindness of Alyosha's God.

Similarly, Father Paneloux recognizes the particular status of children's suffering within the broader context of general suffering. In the initial stages of the plague, he gives a sermon wherein he identifies the plague as a divine punishment for their sins (Camus, *The Plague* 99). However, in a later sermon he is forced to directly confront the problem of the suffering of children.

The difficulty began when we looked into the nature of evil, and among things evil he included human suffering. This we had apparently needful pain, and apparently needless pain; we had Don Juan cast into hell, and a child's death. For while it is right that a libertine should be struck down, we see no reason for a child's suffering. And, truth to tell, nothing was more important on earth than a child's suffering, the horror it inspires in us, and the reasons we must find to account for it. In other manifestations of life God made things easy for us and, thus far, our religion had no merit. (Camus, *The Plague*, 223)

Once again, Father Paneloux does not concern himself with "Don Juan," clearly one of Ivan's "Adults." He rationalizes it as a *quid pro quo* for their own decadence, thus making it a logical consummation of the natural principle of justice. The suffering found in punishment had an underlying cause and rationale that justified it. For children, however, no such justification existed, and Father Paneloux, Ivan, and Alyosha find themselves forced to confront this grim reality. The theme of juvenile suffering was a preoccupation of Camus's, and was found in other writings of his (Just Assassins), and in a speech he gave to Dominican monks in 1946 ("I share with you Christians the same revulsion from evil. But I do not share your hope, and I continue to struggle against this universe in which children suffer and die" [Sprintzen 97]). As such, it was very natural to directly respond to the issue raised in *Brothers Karamazov.*

In regards to the second intertextual point, both Father Paneloux and Alyosha differ from Ivan on how to confront the suffering of children, and are both agreed on the necessity of finding a way to do so. Father Paneloux states that "true, the agony of a child was humiliating to the heart and mind, *but that was why we had to come to terms with it*" (Dostoevsky 225, italics are mine). Alyosha's constant struggle to come to terms with it is indicative of a deeper drive, a belief in the necessity of coming to terms with it. Both characters see this reconciliation as an existential necessity. Ivan does not. He wants to "return his ticket" (Dostoevsky 245), and "consciously accepts his dilemma" (Camus, *The Rebel* 53). Far from coming to terms and reconciling the suffering children with some higher order, he desires to "remain with unrequited suffering and unquenched indignation even if [he's] wrong" (Dostoevsky 245).

The third connecting point is made in the eschatological examinations made by both of the characters in their attempt to find this crucial, needed ingredient for "coming to terms" with the suffering of children. In particular, the argument that, in the final hereafter, all will be directly compensated for in what essentially amounts to utilitarian justification is not given much credence by either Alyosha or Father Paneloux. For Alyosha, it is his acquiescence to Ivan's leading inquiry.

> 'Imagine that you yourself are building an edifice of human destiny with the object of making people happy in the finale, of giving them rest and peace at last, but for that you must inevitably and

unavoidably torture just one tiny creature, that same child who was beating her chest with her little fist, and raise your edifice on the foundation of her unrequited tears—would you agree to be the architect of such conditions? Tell me the truth.'

'No, I would not agree,' Alyosha said softly. (Dostoevsky 245)

Father Paneloux arrives at a similar conclusion:

Thus he might easily have assured them that the child's sufferings would be compensated for by an eternity of bliss awaiting him. But how could he give the assurance when, to tell the truth, he knew nothing about it? For who would dare to assert that eternal happiness can compensate for a single moment's suffering? He who asserted that would not be a true Christian, a follower of the Master who knew all the pangs of suffering in his body and his soul. (Camus, *The Plague* 224)

In both cases, a utilitarian resolution is considered insufficient. The "unrequited suffering" must not be simply compensated for, but be completely extirpated. Since doing so physically is impossible, they must fall back on their Christian symbolism, the fourth relational point.

Both Father Paneloux and Alyosha also invoke the sacrifice of Christ as a way to reconcile suffering with some sense of purpose. Alyosha's laconic replies to his brother's near-monologue in the chapters "Rebellion" and "The Grand Inquisitor" leave much room for interpretation. However, his response of near the end of "Rebellion" gives an insight into his perspective on the issue:

You asked just now if there is in the whole world a being who could and would have the right to forgive. But there is such a being, and he can forgive everything, forgive all and for all, because he himself gave his innocent blood for all and for everything. You've forgotten about him, but it is on him that the structure is being built, and it is to him that they will cry out: 'Just art thou, O Lord, for thy ways have been revealed!' (Dostoevsky 246)

This reliance on the sacrifice of Christ as a justification is shared by Father Paneloux. "No, he, Father Paneloux, would keep faith with that great symbol of all suffering, the tortured body on the cross; he would stand fast, with his back to the wall, and face honestly the terrible problem of children's agony" (Camus, *The Plague* 244).

Later on Father Paneloux is more specific about what the Christian symbolism means for the particular case of the suffering of children:

> The love of God is a hard love...yet it alone can reconcile us to the suffering and deaths of children, it alone can justify them, since we cannot understand them, and we can only make God's will ours. That is the hard lesson I would share with you today. That is faith, cruel in men's eyes, and crucial in God's...We must aspire beyond ourselves toward that high and fearful vision. And on that lofty plain all will fall into place, all discords be resolved, and truth flash forth from the seeming cloud of injustice. (Camus, *The Plague* 228)

Critique of Alyosha's Faith

The inevitable question, and the one that marks the point where Camus begins to fill the gaps left by Dostoevsky, is the underlying why behind the belief. Why do they maintain a faith in the face of the difficulties of reconciling the benevolent God with the circumstances around them? As previously mentioned, a reading of Alyosha through Father Paneloux suggests that this belief is pragmatically-based; it is adopted because the alternative is not bearable. There is some direct evidence of this within *The Brothers Karamazov.*

> "As I told you: I just want to drag on until I'm thirty and then— smash the cup on the floor!"
>
> "And the sticky little leaves, and the precious graves, and the blue sky, and the woman you love! How will you live, what will you love them with?" Alyosha exclaimed ruefully. "Is it possible, with such hell in your heart and in your head? No, you're precisely going in order to join them... and if not, you'll kill yourself, you won't endure it!" (Dostoevsky 263)

The reference to suicide—an important theme for Camus—is explicit ("this theme of suicide in Dostoevsky, then, is indeed an absurd theme," Camus, *Myth of Sisyphus* 109). For Alyosha, the pointlessness and absurdity of a universe without purpose is unacceptable (in contrast to Ivan, for whom "absurdities are all too necessary on this earth" [Dostoevsky 243]). Therefore, humankind requires some sense of higher meaning and purpose, which Alyosha finds in his Christian God. This perspective is also supported by the second half of *The Brothers Karamazov*, in which the Godless Ivan goes insane from guilt for the murderous consequences of his atheistic ideology. These thematic elements strongly hint at pragmatic reasons for belief in God but, once again, Dostoevsky's dearth of detail leaves this up to interpretation. The ramifications of the nonexistence of God seems to be given more attention in *The Brothers Karamazov* than the existence of God *per se*.

Camus allows more access to Father Paneloux's thought processes. As the plague progresses, Father Paneloux adopts the all-or-nothing dichotomy presented by Camus in *The Rebel* (52), even going so far as to describing it as one of God's most important virtues (Camus, *The Plague* 225). In this sense, he reflects Camus's affinity for Ivan, whom Camus also represents as having an all-or-nothing attitude. "Having previously been willing to compromise, the slave suddenly adopts an attitude of All or Nothing. Knowledge is born and conscience awakened" (Camus, *The Rebel* 20). In comparing Ivan to the romantics, he writes that "the essential difference is that the romantics allowed themselves to be complacent, while Ivan compelled himself to do evil so as to be coherent" (Camus, *The Rebel* 52). Father Paneloux's all-or-nothing perspective dichotomizes his decisions: to either believe in everything or deny everything (Camus, *The Plague* 223), or to hate God or to love God (225). He responds to this decision like a true religious pragmatist. "Who, among you, I ask, would dare deny everything?"(223), "who would choose to hate [God]?" (225) Father Paneloux is forced into his religious beliefs simply because he cannot tolerate the alternative. He undergoes Kierkegaard's "leap to faith." God and immortality is believed because otherwise all would be absurd; his factual existence is secondary. "Then the ineluctable option, Paneloux's 'all or nothing' imposes itself: either one takes up one's abode, in the Absurd and faces up vigorously to the monster, or one must believe in the 'miracle' which amounts to total submission and silence" (Onimus 47).

On a related note, Father Paneloux also demonstrates an epistemological angst that provides a commentary on Alyosha's own situation. His private monologue to himself frankly admits an ignorance of the hereafter (Camus, *The Plague* 224) after his initially simplistic faith is dramatically shaken by the death of Othon's son.

However, Alyosha is seemingly quite sure of his own faith. On the last page of *The Brothers Karamazov*, Alyosha assures the schoolchildren near him, "certainly we shall rise, certainly we shall see and gladly, joyfully tell one another all that has been" (Dostoevsky, 776). Furthermore, Camus admits that Dostoevsky stated that "the immortality of the human soul exists without a doubt" (Camus, *Myth of Sisyphus* 110). However, Camus is openly suspicious of this firm belief, and demonstrates bewilderment at Alyosha's definitive statements regarding the factuality of religious belief:

Dostoevsky wrote "the chief question that will be pursued throughout this book is the very one from which I have suffered consciously or unconsciously all life-long: the existence of God." It is hard to believe that a novel sufficed to transform into joyful certainty the suffering of a lifetime. One commentator correctly pointed out that Dostoevsky is on Ivan's side and that the affirmative chapters took three months of effort whereas what he called "the blasphemies" were written in three weeks in a state of excitement. (Camus, *Myth of Sisyphus* 111)

Far from accepting Alyosha's confessions of faithfulness, he saw in the narrative of the Karamazovs a deeper struggle within the psyche of Dostoevsky over the existence of God, a struggle that found its manifestation in the skeptical believer of Father Paneloux, a projection of a more sincere, genuine Alyosha, perhaps an attempt to bring to the surface what he saw as Dostoevsky's admitted "unconscious" questioning of the existence of God.

Like Ivan, both Alyosha and Father Paneloux are forced to accept the "dilemma, to be virtuous and illogical, or logical and criminal" (Camus, *The Rebel* 53). In accepting the all-or-nothing paradigm, the pragmatic religionists in this case are in some way accepting some of Camus's basic premises. "The Jesuit Paneloux has adopted a position resembling the third-century Tertullian's *credo quia absurdum est*--I believe because it is absurd-- a position closer to Camus's own absurdist vision" (Kellman 58). By creating a sympathetic character (perhaps "perhaps the most sympathetically drawn to Christian in all of Camus's fiction" [Sprintzen 94]). that operates out of his own existentialist principles and that is a literary mimicry of Alyosha, Camus is recognizing the legitimacy of Dosteovsky's questions.

However, even though Father Paneloux utilizes absurdist concepts and vocabulary, he varies from Camus in his final decision. In this way, Camus attempts to problematize Alyosha's perspective on faith; seeing it as the strongest case to be made for faith (operating, as it does, out of many of Camus's own absurdist principles), he attempts to discredit it, directly confronting Dostoevsky's nascent Christian existentialism. In *The Plague,* Rieux and Tarrau have a conversation that addresses the issue of belief for the sake of meaning.

> "After all," the doctor repeated, then hesitated again, fixing his eyes on Tarrou, "it's something that a man of your sort can understand most likely, but, since the order of the world is shaped by death, mightn't it be better for God if we refuse to believe in Him and struggle with all our might against death, without raising our eyes towards the heaven where He sits in silence?" Tarrou nodded. "Yes. But your victories will never be lasting: that's all." Rieux's face darkened. "Yes, I know that. But it's no reason for giving up the struggle." "No reason, I agree. Only, I now can picture what this plague must mean for you." "Yes, a never ending defeat." (128)

According to Belford "it is probably Rieux who comes closest to the author at this time in his life" (97). In this case, Rieux's perspective is essentially Camus's. While Camus agrees with the initial existential setup ascribed to these character's cosmologies, he ultimately disagrees with the pragmatic argument for religious belief. He, unlike Father Paneloux, "dare[s] to deny everything" (Dostoevsky 223). In one of his commentaries on the matter, he directly "accuses Dostoevsky of betraying the absurd by using it...as a springboard to faith. He classes Dostoevsky as a Christian existentialist novelist who makes the illogical 'saut.'" (Davison 17-18), and that therefore he does not qualify as a complete absurdist (Camus, *Myth of Sisyphus* 111).

There is a final disconnect between Alyosha and Father Paneloux found in the ultimate fate of their characters. While we are not told whether his corpse was still clasping his crucifix (as had been his habit), and while, in an earlier version of the story, Paneloux completely loses his faith (Gray 169), it does appear that, like Alyosha, he ends his role in the story as a man of faith. However, it is strongly hinted at that his succumbing was the result of his decision to follow the God-who-allows-the-suffering-of-children. He does not show any of the specific symptoms of the disease, and when he dies the card next to his bed reads "doubtful case" (Camus, *The Plague* 234). Cordes (67) shares this interpretation when he writes about Paneloux's last moments:

> He was extremely restless and, perhaps because of his denial of the personality, he appeared "more dead than alive." Moreover he coughed constantly as if he were trying to regurgitate something that was choking him and that he could no longer hold in. …Those who "died" from the plague did so because they succumbed to Evil and to the dehumanization of the absurd rather than heed to the heart's cries. Paneloux endured a similar depersonalization by worshipping the "Genius of the Plague."

Additionally, near his end he regurgitates a clot of red matter, perhaps suggesting a reverse eucharist in which, instead of consuming the blood of Christ, it is vomited up. A death that is caused by an attachment to a God who seemingly does not care about suffering is the exact opposite of what happens in *The Brothers Karamazov,* where it is the atheist that accepts the pointlessness of the universe that leads to a death. While Alyosha tells Ivan that "he'll kill himself" (Dostoevsky 263) because of his beliefs, it is Father Paneloux that dies because of his beliefs. The pragmatic argument for religious belief leads to the kinds of problems for Father Paneloux that its adoption is supposed to ameliorate for Alyosha. Recognizing the absurd for what it is, although painful, would have been less problematic for Father Paneloux than inducing cognitive dissonance by attempting to maintain a belief in a kind God in the face of evidence to the contrary. As Alyosha makes a case for the untenability of unbelief (as Father Paneloux does in the beginning), the ultimate fate of Father Paneloux makes the case for the untenability of forcing belief for the sake of belief in something.

Bibliography

Camus, Albert. *The Myth of Sisyphus.* Trans. Anthony Bower. New York: Alfred A. Knopf, 1954.

Camus, Albert. *The Plague.* Trans. Stuart Gilbert. New York: Vintage, 1991.

Camus, Albert. *The Rebel.* Trans. Justin O'Brien. New York: Alfred A. Knopf, 1958.

Davison, Ray. *Camus, the Challenge of Dostoevsky.* Exeter, UK: University of Exeter Press, 1997.

Dostoevsky, Fyodor. *The Brothers Karamazov.* Trans. Richard Pevear and Larissa Volokhonsky.   New York: Farrar, Straus and Giroux, 2002.

Gray, Margeret E. "Layers of meaning in *La Peste.*" *The Cambridge Companion to Camus.* Ed. Hughes, Edward J. New York: Cambridge University Press, 2007.

Hawkins, Anne Hunsaker. "Editor's Preface." *Literature and Medicine.* 21.1, 2002.

Kellman, Steven G. *The Plague, Fiction and Resistance.* New York: Twayne Publishers, 1993. .

Onimus, Jean. *Albert Camus and Christianity.* Trans. Emmett Parker. Tuscaloosa, AL: University of Alabama Press, 1970.

Sprintzen, David. *Camus: A Critical Examination.* Philadelphia: Temple University Press, 1988

The Absurd Sun

By Kurt Blankschaen

Interpretation of the image of the sun in Camus' work is often tied to either geography or politics. Scholars such as Micheline Tisson-Braun, Alba Amoia, and John Erickson all make the claim that Camus uses the sun to round off the geography of his setting or to make a point about the consequences of actions in Algeria. Later scholars—William Manly, A.D. Nuttall, and Peter Schofer—continue the emphasis of the sun as a geographic role, utilize the sun as part of an internal ambivalence constituting Meursault's frame of mind during the murder, or establish the sun as a literary metaphor for death. These views stem not only from his essays "The Minotaur" and "Summer in Algiers," but also from Camus' literary works, specifically *The Stranger*. These interpretations miss out on the application of the sun as truth in Camus' larger philosophy of the Absurd. The benefit of reconfiguring the sun as a new metaphor for truth—a metaphor of revolt—is that it extrapolates and elevates literary or biographical themes of the Absurd from *The Stranger* to a larger and clearer picture of Camus' philosophy.

Camus uses the sun in *The Stranger* as an Absurdist revolt against the Platonic paradigm of truth as reason. *The Myth of Sisyphus* acts as a background for the larger and more philosophical themes of *The Stranger* and allows Camus' philosopher of the Absurd to emerge. A consequence of this philosophical emergence is the transition from geography, politics, or psychology to a more philosophical grounding. This change allows a window for Camus to develop his Absurdism to cancel, not the idea of truth, but the idea of a rational truth. "Rational truth" here means something that is verifiable through deductive logic; it is detached, objective, and analytic. The "new" Absurdist truth is that human actions are projected into an indifferent universe and is only understood after an experience with Camus' fundamental question of philosophy (suicide). Confronted with Camus' observation, which strips truth of its' Platonic rationale, readers are poised to recast the significance of death which hitherto has dominated Existential discourse. Death, far from instigating a state of anxiety or dread because humans have not fully exercised freedom or choice, is simply a reminder that choices—which sum up existence—are only in the present. The future, like the past, is unalterable insofar as it does not exist.

Absurdity and Previous Conceptions of Light

The philosophical underpinnings of the Absurd first find ground in the opening lines of *The Myth of Sisyphus*: "There is but one truly serious philosophical problem, and that is suicide. Judging whether life is or is not worth living amounts to answering the fundamental question of philosophy. All the rest...comes afterwards" (Camus 3). The conception of the Absurd rooted well enough in two maxims of Existentialism, (1) Absurdism begins by questioning life, not a pre-existing life, a thing either exists or it does not, and (2) the Absurd question does not target a human nature, nor human conditions, but rather *the condition* of human existence. Dr. David Carroll, a professor of French literarture, clarifies this distinction by stating that "What is thus most serious in philosophy, its very condition, is life itself—whatever life is and whatever it ultimately means. All the rest is secondary, frivolous, nothing more than a game—or much worse, dogmatism" (55). The philosophy of the Absurd posits an ironic interaction between a passionate creative human and an indifferent world.

The Myth of Sisyphus was not an introduction to Camus' philosophy; it was, rather, a way to ease people to an Absurd mindset. The work itself gives instances of how people encounter the Absurd in everyday life: The Don Juan (69-77), the artist (77-84), the conqueror (84-92), or the realization that life has become mechanized and routine (12-13). The Absurd in *The Myth of Sisyphus* is personal and relatable; it comes after a long time of normality and strikes with the question "why?" Suddenly the reasons previously given, which had guided actions, no longer seems relevant or right; Camus presents the only two possible options: "Suicide or recovery" (13). Absurdism in *The Myth of Sisyphus* and *The Stranger* gives a larger picture between what Sartre reiterated as Camus' desire to make the distinction "Between the *notion* and the *feeling* of the absurd" (9-10). Both works are intimately linked for Sartre, as "*The Myth of Sisyphus* might be said to aim at giving us this *idea,* and *The Stranger* at giving us the feeling. The order in which the two works appeared seems to confirm this hypothesis. *The Stranger,* the first to appear, plunges us without comment into the 'climate' of the absurd; the essay then comes and illumines the landscape" (10). David O'Connell, a professor of French literature, supports this distinction and informs us that, "Camus wrote that his purpose [for *Sisyphus*] was to deal with an absurd sensitivity...and not with an absurd philosophy" (11), which suggests that the philosophical side of Camus is in his literature.

Camus demonstrates the primacy of literature in *The Myth of Sisyphus,* "The writer has given up telling 'stories' and creates his universe. The great novelists are philosophical novelists—that is, the contrary of thesis writers. For instance, Balzac, Sade, Melville, Stendhal, Dostoevsky, Proust, Malraux, Kafka, to cite but a few" (101). While *Sisyphus* may provide the context to truly appreciate Camus' other works, it offers the heart of Absurdism: "Understanding of the world involves the reduction of that world to a human dimension; for a world that can be explained even with bad reasons is a familiar world and one in which people can survive" (O'Connell 11). What Camus sets out to do in *Sisyphus* is to examine if the reasons given for existence are fact or farce.

Bombarded with the message that choices resonate throughout time, the human condition has been conditioned to stand on a metaphysical platform which offers morals and purpose. But what Camus uncovers in *Sisyphus* is a simple, but jarring, honesty of the human condition. Humans exist like Sisyphus, perpetually rolling a rock up a hill. Sisyphus' routine need not be seen as punishment, however, but rather as a descriptive statement of how reality functions. The universe, for Camus, is "Neither sterile nor futile" (123) but simply is. By describing the world as Absurd and recognizing the limits of reason within that world, Camus desires that his readers do not end up not pitying Sisyphus. When Sisyphus is placed in the Absurd context, Camus writes that people "Must imagine Sisyphus as happy" (123). When humans recognize how actions register and how the human condition functions, previous limits and constraints wither and freedom expands.

One reading of Absurdism rejecting dogmatism is that it is revolting against religious dogmatism. Absurdism rejects a pre-existing meaning in existence from God or some other metaphysical entity. But in context with other Existentialist propositions—specifically Sartre's, humans are condemned to choose, about choice—Camus' rejection of dogmatism would include a rejection of choice as the highest expression of human reason. The belief in a human project that pursues freedom, which only terminates in more freedom, is predicated on reason. It is only after rationally understanding human conditions that choices expand. Before humans can build, they must first understand with what they are building. Choice advances hand-in-hand with reason, but it is precisely this project which Camus undermines in *The Stranger*.

It would be wrong to read Camus' Absurdism as positing no meaning in life. Rather the Absurd undercuts Sartre's emphasis on choice with the rationale that the world is ultimately indifferent to human choices. Humans impose a rational ordering of the world, but the world itself is not rational, it simply is. Before going on to a new interpretation of the sun, it is necessary to examine some of the previous interpretations of it in Camus. Scholar Micheline Tisson-Braun, who grounds her work in the task of tracing "The lyrical current that springs forth in his [Camus] youth, persists underground in his theoricizing period...and timidly reappears later on in an inconclusive new trend, abruptly interrupted by Camus' death" (42). Her work, therefore, is extrapolating the personal Camus to the literary Camus. She begins by foregrounding a hard-to-pin-down—"Pantheistic" (43) in her own words—sense of the divine: "On the very threshold of Camus' poetic universe, the gods are present. They dwell in 'the desert.' Not the actual Sahara, several hundred miles south of Algiers, but the arid, luminous Mediterranean shores of Camus' childhood" (42) which is reiterates to her twofold objective, that Camus' inspiration and literary aim is biographical and geographical.

The sun, given Tisson-Braun's context, takes on a personal or terrestrial importance; "A raging sun was streaming like a rain of fire during the mother's funeral—a premonition of divine vengeance. It came back with blinding fury on the beach where the murder of the Arab took place" (50-51), and so Tisson-Braun's analysis frames the sun in terms of justice within her personal/geographic context. The personal could lead to a post-colonial/political reading; Dr. John Erickson, a French professor, notes that Camus did write favorably of the French during the Algerian Civil War (73). Additionally, the sun functions as a kind of divine agent of justice—a sense of "balance" is restored (Tisson-Braun 51)—the death of the Arab balancing to the death of Maman.

Another scholar, Alba Amoia, argues that geography plays a larger role in how Camus constructed his works: "The names of many great writers are linked with the places they were born or lived, or which they recreated for us in their works" (56). While his place of growing up undoubtedly influenced him, Camus, for Amoia, is a great writer, who is great because of what he is able "To tell us is of universal, not merely local, significance" (56). Indeed, "Camus was infinitely more than a merely 'local' or colonial' writer. He was, in the widest sense, a citizen of the world, and his message was and is addressed to all people everywhere" (56), but despite this appeal to universality, Amoia still frames a discussion of the role of the sun in terms of geography. "The blinding North African sun, the tang of the Mediterranean, permeate much of his work, and the pictures of his native land and its people that he has left us will survive as unique witness to their time and place" (56). Camus is universal, but only as a visitor or a writer, not a philosopher.

Amoia, because she focuses on the importance Camus' travels (57), further solidifies the role of the sun in setting or authenticity of an author representing a homeland, not an author making a philosophical point. This is evident when she says that "Sun and light...are symbols of truth and a source of strength for Camus. This is true even in philosophical terms since his concept of the absurd takes him back full circle to the sun" (58). The role of the sun may be one of strength for Camus, but Amoia frames this strength as physical convalescence. The rustic Mediterranean landscape has a certain kind of power for Camus' novels, but this interpretation of the sun in Camus' works is more a biographical notation and at any rate, it couches the conception of truth in a geographic location (Amoia 59-61).

Amoia is not alone in this conceptualization, as William M. Manly, an English professor, states that "It has been generally observed that Camus' recurring imagery of the sea and sun is derived in large measure from a boyhood spent on the North African littoral, and that his retrospective nostalgia for the barbaric, physical, world of the Algerians is reflected throughout his personal essays and novels" (87). The "philosophical terms" Amoia references are the juxtaposition of place and psychology of place for Camus; places seem dreary or melancholy until they resemble Algeria, then they become vibrant and full of life.

While previous scholarship has examined the symbol of the sun in *The Stranger* as a relationship to geography, setting, or internal ambivalence, the argument presented here is that the sun's presence actually demonstrates a philosophical point: that despite the citadels of reason built around choice, they all come crumbling down in the face of the Absurd and an indifferent world. Time and again light does not guide the characters in *The Stranger*, but in fact "malfunctions" in the rationale for their decisions.

While there is much to be mined from a post-colonial or political reading of the sun in *The Stranger* or the rest of Camus, the focus of this essay is to examine the significance of the sun when placed into the metaphor of light as understanding. John Erickson argues in an essay on Camus that Camus best belongs in "The tradition of French Orientalism" (73), which after invoking Edward Said's name a few lines after, makes the reading more political than philosophical. Said, a towering figure in colonial/postcolonial studies, argues in *Orientalism* that Western attempts to understand native populations in the Middle East, Africa, and India through literature, culture, religion, and anthropology, were in fact subversive and harmful. Colonialist impulses fixed native populations to static and simplified conceptions of colonized ways of life. The sun takes on a stronger political importance because of Erickson's position that Camus is an Orientalist; he writes not to expose an authentic Algerian point of view, but, instead, Camus writes as an ambivalent French "Superimposition" (74), that caricatures Algeria as an exotic or rustic landscape caught up in the romance of the desert under the Algerian sun.

Erickson is right when he says that "The Algerian sun serves as an integral factor in the act of murder which will lead, in Part 2, to the trial and impending execution of Meursault", but his analysis loses focus when he resigns the sun as "An elemental motif in Camus' 'Algerian' novels" (75). There is a deeper point about the sun in *The Stranger* and links the significance of the sun to the deaths, "The description of the events surrounding the funeral is fraught with images of heat and light...during the procession, the oppressive heat...contribute[s] to the extreme discomfort of Meursault and causes his eyes and thoughts to grow blurred" (74-5). Erickson, here, is simply taking note of instances where the sun shows up in scenes. When he does assign meaning to the sun, he asserts that the sun produces discomfort, unhappiness, alienation, and death (75), but he does not break away from the post-colonial or geographic landscape commentary of Camus as an Orientalist. Erickson believes that the sun is part of a larger theme of Camus' "Algerian works" (75-76) and an integral part of Algeria is the sun. "Camus' 'Algerian' novels depict a harsh landscape representative of the North African littoral is both obvious and tangential to the question of how he represented the Maghrebian East in his work" (Erickson 76). While these arguments all tap into powerful political commentary on literary representations of places and people, they neglect an examination of the philosophical importance of the sun as a background for the absurdity of choice as reason which would demonstrate an unconcealed assessment of Absurdity.

A.D. Nuttall, an English professor at Oxford, examines the events in *The Stranger,* specifically the death scenes, with an eye for Meursault's murder motive. "Meursault, surprised to see the Arab again, grips the gun in his pocket and halts under the fierce sun. The tension rises, and the heat grows more oppressive, reminding Meursault of the heat at his mother's funeral, until at last he irrationally takes a step forward" (104). Nuttall's reading of the murder scene does a terrific job of collecting what is going on and provides keen insight into Meursault—the heat at the death of the Arab is the same as the heat during Maman's funeral—but by focusing on the consequences and variables of the murder, Nuttall's assessment remains literary and eschews the philosophical. For instance, "During the incident his [Meursault's] head was full of the light and heat of the sun, of feelings of oppression, flickering anxiety and memory, awareness of a knife drawn before him, desperation...The problem which now rises is this: does the second story [which I have quoted] exonerate Meursault?" (104). Nuttall provides a fine character analysis, but it does not extrapolate Meursault's action to the larger philosophy of the Absurd.

Peter Schofer, a French professor, offers a different view for the interplay between Meursault and light. He first introduces Cruikshank's interpretation, that the light acted as a sort of hallucination for Meursault and that the death scenes run as a double text of past as present and life and death (132-33), but then adds that the entire novel can be read as a double text. Schofer assigns the sun during both death scenes as an inspiration for movement for Meursault: "In the first case, movement is like life—we move on. In the second, Meursault causes death when he can go no further" (134). But Schofer's interpretation, an updated version of Cruikshank's "double text", necessitates swallowing a psychological assessment of Meursault which rebuffs the Absurd. "In both scenes, nature is alive and humans act as though they were death. Meursault acts as though he were dead at the funeral, because on a real level he does not come to terms with death; it remains no more than signs. This realization only comes to the surface at the instant that he shoots the Algerian, transforming his repressed grief into violence" (135). Such a reading does not fit into the larger picture of the

Absurd, as Meursault does not grieve not because he does not accept Maman's death, but because he does not grieve in a traditional social way. He smokes his cigarette not because he wants to escape Maman's death, but because he wanted to smoke a cigarette. Furthermore, if the Arab's murder was a catharsis of grief over Maman, Meursault could have said this at the interrogation, the trial, or the attempt at conversion and all would have been right. He would not have been compromising his character, but would have been honest and consistent with the Absurd context Camus framed *The Stranger* in. Schofer is right to link the deaths and the suns as major points in *The Stranger*, but he misses the mark for why they are important.

Interpreting the sun as a larger philosophical idiom is not simply replacing one symbolism with another. It elevates Camus to a serious philosopher. The sun is an idiom because it enables intelligibility for the rest of the philosophy of the Absurd. *The Stranger* may be the marquee demonstration of the Absurd, but Camus discusses the importance of Absurdism and its consequences in other works. The previously quoted section of *Sisyphus*, for instance, where Camus avers that truly great works of literature rise to the philosophical. "The writer has given up telling 'stories' and creates his universe. The great novelists are philosophical novelists—that is, the contrary of thesis writers. For instance, Balzac, Sade, Melville, Stendhal, Dostoevsky, Proust, Malraux, Kafka, to cite but a few" (101). If the sun is only a literary or biographical symbol, Camus remains a good writer and story teller. But if the sun is a philosophical truth, then Camus is a great novelist and philosopher. In short, the philosophical and Absurd sun recognizes Camus for what he is.

The Sun as Absurdist truth: Maman

Camus starts *The Stranger* off with a death. "Maman died today. Or yesterday maybe, I don't know. I got a telegram from the home: 'Mother deceased. Funeral tomorrow. Faithfully yours.' That doesn't mean anything. Maybe it was yesterday" (3). Camus takes a monumental event in life, the death of a parent, and shows a deep level of detachment from it. The removal from the event is seen in his lack of concern towards his mother. Today, yesterday, the day before, it really does not matter. Initially, a reader may find such removal disturbingly cold and distant, but the point, of course, for Camus is that knowing the date of death does not change the facticity of death. Equally so, knowledge, in the traditional sense begets mourning.

Discovery of a death, especially a parent's, sinks deep in people. Yet Meursault does not grieve, and this is symptomatic of a larger character trait: "Meursault has desires and affects but no sentiments. He has neither memory nor projects, and his synthetic faculties do not operate above the immediate physical level" (Tisson-Braun 49). This comes out in Meursault in the way he interacts with people at the funeral, including his desire to smoke a cigarette (8-11), his desire to see Marie, not to be consoled but to have fun, after the funeral (19-20) and his indifference to his boss' offer of a job in Paris (41). Camus' point again is made: mourn or do not mourn, an event—however tragic—has occurred and nothing can be done to alter that fact. If Meursault did or did not wail at the loss of his mother, his mother remains lost.

The very first word Camus uses for the scene, "Maman," a child's word for mother, has deep implications (Ward vii). Grief is largely a social construction; society has set guidelines for how people grieve the loss of a loved one. The social process of grieving forgoes that it is not society, but the individual, who must cope with the loss. But even this analysis assumes death as a loss. Meursault does not mourn his mother, not because he does not love her or feel attached to her, but a possible explanation could be that in his child-view of his mother—as evidenced by "Maman"—Meursault has not acculturated to the process of socially grieving. But saying a child does not understand death and is not sad in the same way an adult is sad at the death of a loved one, misses the vocabulary nuance and Camus' point; perhaps a child does understand death better and so does not put ashes on his head or remain housebound for a designated number of weeks or stay single out of respect for a specified number of years. A child carries on with life as it comes in the present, and so Meursault lives life as it comes to him. "He registers facts, but not their meanings; his consciousness is purely instantaneous; he lacks the principle of unity and continuity that characterizes man" (Tisson-Braun 49). Readers may take Meursault's detachment from his mother's death as cold or inhuman; his mind registers that Maman is dead, but it does not attach meaning because there is no inherent meaning for his mind to attach to. Meursault could grieve lugubriously or not at all, either way, the meaning of his mother's death comes into play only when he has created it. Each moment of the present leads to the future, never the past.

The final scene of Maman's death brings a motif Camus implements throughout the novel to contrast light with Absurdity (15-18). Plato, an extremely influential Greek philosopher, in his work *The Republic*, is credited with establishing the metaphor of sight equaling understanding. The Myth of the Cave sets up a scenario where people are held captive in a cave and are ultimately kept captive by a mixture of their own cowardice, apathy, or ignorance and their captors who entertain them with shadow puppet shows (Plato 205-06). "The truth" Plato informs us, "Would be literally nothing but the shadows of the images" (206) for the prisoners in the cave. Immediately there is the Platonic vocabulary that objects and truths in this world are only shadows of others. But the real philosophical importance comes when a prisoner is freed and leaves the cave: after exiting and adjusting to the light, the former prisoner's "Eye is turned towards more real existence, he has a clearer vision" (Plato 206), which brings sight equivalent to understanding, because it is only with a clear vision that real existence can be understood.

But Plato realizes that this is not an all at once event; it takes time to realize the Platonic paradigm of knowledge. The former prisoner "Will require time to grow accustomed to the sight of the upper world. And first he will see the shadows best, next the reflections of men and other objects in the water, and then the objects themselves" (Plato 206). Finally, the former prisoner arrives at the last object, the sun, which allows him to "See him in his own proper place, and not in another; and he will contemplate him as he is" (Plato 207). With this last piece in place, Plato reaches the apex of his philosophy, the ability to think of things in themselves. All of this is made possible by the light of the sun, which is called "good" in Plato's philosophy. It is important to note, however, that "good" is not good in a moral or ethical sense, but rather it is good insofar as it makes all other truths intelligible. When people understand or see something in mathematics, politics, or virtue, it is only because that the sun—understanding— made it possible. Plato's theory of truth, sun, and importance of sight, are towering philosophical symbols which have been incorporated into a myriad of different expressions. Camus is no exception insofar as he adopts it, but where Camus differs, and really takes off in his own philosophical vein, is that he undercuts Plato's aim and topples the Platonic paradigm.

While Plato is credited with marrying sight and understanding, he also extends the scope of rational truth to music. Music, for Plato, was not a rhapsodic expression of emotion or some improvisionational syncopation; it was the rigid mathematical construction of sound. Math professor Morris Kline, author of *Mathematics for the Nonmathematician,* which acts as a history of math, provides the historical context for Plato's utilization of music. "As the eyes are made for astronomy so are the ears made for the motion which produces harmony: and thus we have two sister sciences, as the Pythagoreans teach, and we assent" (436). The concern about Platonic astronomy is not so much as thought of today—the Greeks pursued astronomy so as to perpetuate a specific Greek assessment of mathematical aesthetics (Kline 23 & 171)—but instead is linked with the Pythagorean emphasis on a kind of transcendent nature of math; mathematics underwrites both astronomical movement and musical formation, along with many other manifestations. Though the Pythagorean conception of music and Plato's conception of music are similar, they are not a one-to-one translation; the Pythagoreans placed prominence on how music sounded whereas Plato focused more on the mathematical principles built into the musical harmonies. Music was beautiful to Plato not because of its physical acoustics or pleasantries, but because it was rigidly constructed and followed a deductive precision; music, like sight, allowed physical access to a higher rational truth. Music, therefore, is another physical representation of a rational Platonic truth.

While his Myth of the Cave has specific philosophic consequences, Plato's observation of truth as light finds corroboration in everyday language: "Do you see?" "Is this clear?" "I'm in the dark," "Clear as day," "She is a bright student," and numerous others, all rely on the metaphor of light as some kind of understanding. Camus uses this linguistically embedded metaphor to drive home his point of the Absurdity in human effort. Perez, Maman's lover, follows the funeral procession despite his limp. As the procession proceeds, Perez falls more and more behind. Meursault, keeping with his detached personality, notices "That for quite some time the countryside had been buzzing with the sound of insects and the crackling of grass" (16). He also notices the increasing speed of the procession (16). He responds ambiguously to a question about his mother's age, it would not really matter if he knew or not, and realizes all of this under the sweltering heat of the sun. Camus saturates this scene with light: "I was surprised at how fast the sun was climbing in the sky", the countryside was "Flooded with sunlight" and "The glare from the sky was unbearable" (16) and so he sets the stage for futility.

Absurdity asserts that choice can be dressed up in reason or some other sacrosanct justification, but in the end, choices register in a world that is indifferent. On the one hand, Meursault is attending his mother's funeral procession with no conventional or traditional desire—not to moan or grieve—to be there. On the other, Perez is desperately attempting to be in the picture. As the sun—truth—increases, Perez falls behind and tries to reconnect with the funeral train. Though his attempts are noble (a limping elderly man going across countryside) they do not mean anything in the final analysis; he faints when the procession finally gets to the church (18). The truth of the matter is that Perez's efforts amount to nothing. He tries so hard to be at the funeral that he passes out from exhaustion by the time he achieves his goal. Perez's efforts are not squandered in the truest sense of the word, they simply do not matter. The burial would have still happened whether he was there or not. The burial then, acts as a sort of metaphor for understanding human actions in the Absurd. Like Plato, it is through the sun, but in a vastly different way, that this truth is known. The truth of Absurdity—that human actions are projected into an indifferent universe—becomes known through the oppressive heat. Though Meursault and Perez both have the same goal, to be at the funeral, one is expending much more energy, and yet the same result occurs.

Camus' Absurdity reaches its zenith in this moment because just as the sun physically saps the strength, so too do the attempts to construct meaning physically tire the human spirit. Humans are physical yes, but they are also social and intellectual as well. The need to create meaning requires a concerted effort to create. But this effort, demonstrated by the bootlessness of Perez, is ultimately futile. Ceremonies which once held value to us as children lose importance with age. The need to re-create is always present, and the simple fact of recreating meaning means humans must join Perez as he limps across the countryside in the oppressive heat. But as futile as this attempt to create meaning may be, humans nevertheless keep on creating. Human efforts, like Perez's may not amount to anything, but still people try. Camus castes his Absurdity in intense light because it represents the unhidden truth of life; choice, condition, or anything else all melt away under the intense heat of this sun, this truth. Choice will always choose to express condition, but life still goes on whether or not a person chooses. A person can construct whatever she likes, but in the end, it really only mattered to her. Even that final consolation is not always guaranteed. Perez realizes the fools errand he is on: "Big tears of frustration and exhaustion were streaming down his cheeks" (18), but despite his impotent chagrin, Perez continues to try and so illustrates Camus' Absurdity in action.

The Sun and the Arab

The theme of the Absurd underwriting existence permeates the novel and emerges again in full force about halfway through his work as Meursault shoots an Arab who stabbed his friend Raymond. In the pages preceding the Arab's death, there is more interplay between the sun and reason metaphor. Meursault puts trust in the power of the sun/reason/choice when he, Masson, and Raymond start talking, "I was absorbed by the feeling that the sun was doing me a lot of good" (50). Notice the word choice of "feeling" here, because it underscores the importance of the sun as a malfunctioning reason of choice; people feel that choice is tied up in reason when the Absurd reality is that it is not.

The confrontation between Meursault, Raymond, Masson, and the Arabs takes place when "The sun was shining almost directly overhead onto the sand, and the glare on the water was unbearable" (Camus 52). Not only is the event taking place in broad daylight, but the sunlight is intensified by the interaction with the water. The understanding is magnified with the light; it is also reflected away from the world. After the initial attack, where Raymond is wounded, he and Meursault return to hunt out the Arabs. "By now, the sun was overpowering. It shattered into little pieces on the sand and water" (Camus 55), which is symbolic foreshadowing of the reasons Meursault gives to not shoot the Arab.

Camus' use of the sun continues throughout the confrontation, and until the men are done sizing each other up, "There was nothing but the sun and the silence" (55). While Raymond breaks the silence by asking Meursault if he can shoot the Arab, Meursault responds with "reasons" which answer Raymond but seem horribly inadequate, especially because it is Meursault who shoots the Arab later on. "Should I let him have it?" Raymond asks, to which Meursault responds "He hasn't said anything yet. It'd be pretty lousy to shoot him like that" (Camus 56). But the question and answer session is not done yet, because Raymond informs Meursault that "I'll call him something and when he answers back, I'll let him have it", to which Meursault admonishes Raymond with "'Right. But if he doesn't draw his knife, you can't shoot" (Camus 56). These seem like reasonable answers; people cannot shoot other people who are unarmed and who do not provide provocation, but in reality, these aren't really good reasons. The Arab already attacked Raymond and if he shot him in the heat of the fight it would be called self-defense and juries would be inclined to say that Raymond was in the right. But what Camus is trying to show here is that a few hours, which transforms self-defense to murder, at bottom does not really make a difference.

A subtle but important note in this scene that "The sun glinted off Raymond's gun as he handed it to me" (Camus 56) and with that transfer of gun and truth Meursault realizes that "You could either shoot or not shoot" (Camus 56). But the choice slips away from him for the moment, as the Arabs depart. Meursault walks Raymond back to the bungalow, "But the heat was so intense that it was just as bad standing still in the blinding stream falling from the sky. To stay or go, it amounted to the same thing" (Camus 57). Meursault is not making this decision out of passion or guilt for not fighting the Arab when he attacked Raymond. Harkening back to Plato and truth as light, he is overwhelmed by light, surrounded in every way, both by light and by heat, and in this context of absolute submersion he makes his decision to go, which amounted to the same as staying (Camus 57).

Following through with his decision to go back to the beach, different kinds of interplay with the light metaphor emerge. "I was walking slowly toward the rocks and I could feel my forehead swelling under the sun" (Camus 57), as he approaches the beach to make his fateful decision, Meursault is penetrated and oversaturated with light. The over-abundance of light should usually signify an informed decision or a decision couched in calculated reason. But the Arab's murder is anything but rational or calculated. Camus ties this abundance of light into his Absurdity: "With every blade of light that flashed off the sand, from a bleached shell or a piece of broken glass, my jaw tightened" (57). What is important to notice here is that the light reflects off of the world. Just as humans pour calculated choices into an indifferent world, so does the light project itself into the world. In both cases, light and choices, however, do not remain in the world. The light is reflected back and choice does not stick. In the face of this humans nevertheless tighten their jaws and strain their muscles to redouble their efforts in projecting choices onto the world.

The light metaphor reaches fever pitch with the death of the Arab. The significance of the Arab's death is not as terse as Maman's, and Camus continues with the light motif with intense imagery of the sun to amplify the truth value of his Absurdist principle. The hot sun blurred Meursault's vision: he no longer saw an Arab, a human being, Meursault only saw "A form shimmering before [his] eyes in the fiery air" (58). Note the Platonic idiom of "form" here. The Arab is now an abstraction, the form of a human. In this context of pure sunlight, nothing should, according to the Platonic paradigm of light as reason, come between Meursault and the Arab; Meursault should make the most rational choice. He later takes a step towards the Arab to alleviate the heat, but admonishes himself: "I knew that it was stupid, that I wouldn't get the sun off me by stepping forward. But I took a step, one step, forward" (59). With the truth of the Absurd bearing down on him in the form of a choice, Camus couples the grandiose choice of murder with the mundane choice of taking a step. The consequences to either come to naught, yet Meursault does both.

Camus links the deaths of the Arab and Maman. "The sun was starting to burn my cheeks, and I could feel drops of sweat gathering in my eyebrows. The sun was the same as it had been the day I'd buried Maman" (58-59). The sun now is no longer just an objective factor illuminating the futility of choices, but is in fact reflected by others as futile. Drawing his knife, the Arab reflects and concentrates the suns' rays to Meursault. "The light shot off the steel and it was like a long flashing blade cutting at my forehead" (59). The sun flashing on the knife means that the light is focused; it could be seen as a last attempt to keep reason and choice in the picture for Meursault. But light/reason dancing off the edge of a knife is ultimately overcome by the Absurd.

The sun in this particular scene takes on another dimension. So thoroughly is Meursault penetrated by this truth that the sun transforms from solely a visionary phenomenon and becomes an entirely different quality. "All I could feel were the cymbals of sunlight crashing on my forehead and, indistinctly, the dazzling spear flying up from the knife in front of me" (59). There are two things to notice about this transformation. First, the truth of Absurdity as not merely an intellectual truth—the sun had the properties not only of light, but also of heat, and so also has a physical nature—but a physical truth. The physical nature is demonstrated as the light takes on the additional quality of sound. No longer are Meursault's eyes the only sense in contact with the light, but the light as a cymbal's sound deepens the contact with the truth, which rebuts Plato's assertion that music is a rational manifestation. The second notation follows on the heels of the Arab focusing the sun into an individual level. The sun reflects off the knife no longer as an overall illumination, the light off the knife is now transformed into a light which pierces, which ensures contact with Meursault.

Meursault, like every other human, can never un-see the consequences to an action. With the omnipresence of sun in the general sense and sun as a focused reflection off the Arab's knife, there remains the striking parallel with Plato's cave. Meursault is outside the cave, bathed in the sun and should be making a choice with pure reason. Additionally, his mind is not clouded by loyalty to his friend or a sense of vengeance, and so there is really nothing to impair his sense of judgment. But the fact of the matter is, nothing clouds Meursault's judgment, his choice is made with the knowledge that his choice ultimately registers in an indifferent world. On another level, it is rather cutting that just before Meursault shoots, "The sea carried up a thick, fiery breath. It seemed to [him] as if the sky split open from one end to the other to rain down fire" (59), because it is fire which helps keep people in Plato's Cave. Fire is a sense of light, but not as potent as the sun. Continuing from the perspective that Meursault is carrying on Camus' revolt from the Platonic paradigm, the fire can be seen as one last attempt to keep Meursault in the Cave of Reason, the idea that the universe is rational. Both of the sources of fire come from outside of Meursault's existence, one from the sky, the other from the sea, which is in stark contradiction to Plato and the idea that humans can access intellectual and rational truths internally. On the cusp of overthrowing Plato and the idea of a rational universe, "[His] whole being tensed," (59) which indicates that it was not just the intellectual part of Meursault that struggled with his revolution. He shoots and kills the Arab. The knife falls away. Meursault, through the Absurd, has shot reason dead.

The addition of light as sound is a deep and subtle transformation, one which returns to usurping the Platonic paradigm. Remember that music was rationally ordered for Plato, that each note was selected with careful precision. Music was an expression of a deductive mathematical process, so Camus' use of the cymbal is quite striking. While cymbals can be used in concert with other instruments in a larger musical piece, Camus clearly uses them as a disruption which overwhelms reason and stops the movement. The cymbals clash, they do not compliment. Even so, Plato focused more on the mathematical beauty of music as opposed to the acoustic quality. The clash does not so much break a musical harmony mid beat, but rather shatters the Platonic silence of a mathematical harmony existing only in thought.

On point, Meursault's shots kill not only the Arab, but Plato's, as opposed to Pythagoras', concept of music: "I knew that I had shattered the *harmony* of the day, the exceptional *silence* of a beach where I'd been happy" (59 emphasis added). By breaking the "The harmony of the day, the exceptional silence of a beach," Meursault kills the harmony accomplished by Plato, not Pythagoras. Because Plato simply required mathematical beauty in harmony, it could be expressed in silence and would never have to be performed. Plato's rational conceptualization allows the assurance that things do make sense and that there is a deductive process or a reason for why or how things happen; in essence, a rational conceptualization of music, of thought, of existence, is the beach before the gunshot.

Unsettling as it may be, and this is why the truth must be piercing—to get through—Meursault's action is detached. He felt no special love for Raymond, nor did he act out of overwhelming grief for his mother's death. He did not feel threatened and it even crosses his mind before he fires the gun that he could walk away (58). In fact, Camus does not hide Meursault's motive from us; at the trial when Meursault has had numerous chances to duck behind his mother's death as an excuse, he simply bumbles out that he killed the Arab because of the sun. This reasoning is, to stick with Camus' vocabulary, absurd (with a lower case "a"), but return to the reminder that light is truth—vis-à-vis Plato's Myth of the Cave—and follow the reasoning to the inevitable conclusion that the sun being the source of light stands as that truth which enables all other truths intelligible, then it is possible to draw the conclusion that as Meursault stood before the Arab, he was overtaken not by emotion or some other sense of loss of control, but rather of the overpowering knowledge of the Absurd. Faced with the realization that shooting the Arab or not shooting the Arab still ultimately had the same consequences, Camus demonstrates the far-reaching power of his philosophy.

Conclusion

Camus does not reject the idea of truth. It would be a mistake to take his overturning of Plato's conception of truth as rational as a total rejection of truth. What Camus has done is turned the entire scheme of human construction in on itself. The ultimate nature of truth does not lie on the other side of a divided line, but rather exists in the here and now. The truth of reality, for Camus, is that human actions are no wholly rational. Equally so, actions do not stick in some kind of metaphysical imitation of a form. They are conditioned by existence and emotions, their effects fray as existence ceases. Accepting Camus' Absurd truth makes all other truths intelligible. It elevates his literary works to philosophical works and it ties the larger thrust of the rest of his works together. *The Stranger* denounces Plato's conception of truth, not truth itself.

But what does this revolt of light through Camus mean? Just as Plato's truth about light made all other truths intelligible, so too does Camus' truth about the light of the Absurd make all other truths and actions intelligible in an Absurd world. A cursory assessment might suggest that since humans live in an indifferent universe, choices do not matter. But the fact of the matter is that while the universe may be indifferent to human choices, humans are not indifferent to choices; they are how existence is shaped and how people impress themselves—however futile—into the universe. Though actions may be swept away after death, it is inconsequential to the present, which is the only way of registering choices at all. This does not mean that people should not plan to go to the grocery store tomorrow or to college later in life, but it does mean that those choices can only be made when they arrive, only when the future becomes present. Furthermore, people must accept responsibility, both good and bad, for their choices in the present. What is due in the present cannot be put off until the future. O'Connell offers an Absurd lens to see rightly in the Absurd world: "Once having acknowledged the place of self in time, our logical thought processes will then lead us to think about ourselves with respect to death" (12). Certain things are beyond control—birth and death—but what is done with those things during the time given is not certain.

Existentialism may expound the power of choice, but Camus' sun is a quiet reminder that choice never truly cancels anything. "Deep down I knew perfectly well that it doesn't much matter whether you die at thirty or at seventy, since in either case other men and women will naturally go on living—and for thousands of years. In fact, nothing could be clearer. Whether it was now or twenty years from now, I would still be the one dying" (114). Choice of any caliber may seem to be a fancy exercise of the human will, but it ultimately does not change the outcome of all choices: people still die and life still goes on.

The most monumental choice in one person's life, Meursault's decision to murder another human being, is in the grand scheme of things unimportant. The people his life touched will still move on. France will still execute people, the judge will still try to save people, the defense attorney will still never-mind his clients, and the prosecutor will still try people *ad hominum*. Nothing changed because Meursault shot the Arab. Nothing would have changed had he not shot the Arab. But this does not mean that the power of choice has been stolen away. In fact, quite the contrary, for people still go on choosing because the window in which humans can make choices is limited to their existence in the present. Sartre sums the significance of Camus' recasting of death: "The presence of death at the end of our path has made our future go up in smoke; our life has 'no future'; it is a series of present moments" (14). Camus' discussion of the Absurd Man in *Sisyphus* shows that he recognizes the importance of death, but that it is not as important as others made it out to be. "Assured of his temporally limited freedom, of his revolt devoid of future, and of his mortal consciousness, he lives out his adventure within the span of his lifetime. That is his field, that is his action, which he shields from any judgment but his own. A greater life cannot mean another life" (66). In grounding the power of choice and meaning only within existence, Camus remains in line with much of Existentialism, but it is in the framework of his Absurdity where he deflates the importance of death.

Heidegger, Kierkegaard, or almost any other Existentialist, imposes a sense of urgency, dread, or anxiety in the context of death. The fact that time to create meaning is confined to existence alone is overwhelming, and thus the sense of urgency impels a person's creative capacities. But, as Camus would point out, humans are projecting this anxiety into an indifferent world, and furthermore, death is not something which should induce anxiety or dread. No matter how people trammel their freedom the final outcome of death is unavoidable. Death, instead of a redoubtful unknown, is a reminder that even the most anxiously planned grandiose project, will still only be experienced in the present. Worrying about the future is worrying about something which does not yet exist, and if it does not yet exist, it does not exist. Camus thus undercuts Existential thought which focuses on the future and demonstrates that Existentialism is not a philosophy of the future, but of the present.

Bibliography

Amoia, Alba. "Sun, Sea, and Geraniums: Camus *en voyage*." *Critical Essays on Albert Camus*. Ed. Bettina L. Knapp. Boston: G. K. Hall & Co., 1988. 56-73. Print.

Camus, Albert. *The Stranger*. Trans. Matthew Ward. New York: First Vintage International, 1988. Print.

---*The Myth of Sisyphus*. Trans. O'Brien, Justin. New York: Vintage International, 1955. Print.

Carroll, David. "Rethinking the Absurd: *Le Mythe de Sisyphe*." *The Cambridge Companion to Camus*. Ed. Edward J. Hughes. Cambridge: Cambridge University Press, 2007. Print.

Erickson, John. "Albert Camus and North Africa: A Discourse of Exteriority." *Critical Essays on Albert Camus*. Ed. Bettina L. Knapp. Boston: G. K. Hall & Co., 1988.   73-88. Print.

Manly, William M. "Journey to Consciousness: The Symbolic Pattern of Camus' *L'Etranger*." *Modern Critical Interpretations: Albert Camus' The Stranger*. Ed. Harold Bloom. Philadelphia: Chelsea House Publishers, 2001. 83-94. Print.

Nuttall, A.D. "Did Meursault Mean to Kill the Arab?—The Intentional Fallacy Fallacy." *Modern Critical Interpretations: Albert Camus' The Stranger*. Ed. Harold Bloom. Philadelphia: Chelsea House Publishers, 2001. 95-106. Print.

Plato. *The Republic and Other Works*. Trans. Trans. B Jowett. New York: Anchor Books, 1973. Print.

Rhein, Phillip H. *Albert Camus: Revised Edition*. Ed. David O'Connell. New York: Prentice Hall International, 1989. Print.

Sartre, Jean Paul."An Explication of *The Stranger*." *Modern Critical Interpretations: Albert Camus' The Stranger*. Ed. Harold Bloom. Philadelphia: Chelsea House Publishers, 2001. 95-106. Print.

Schofer, Peter. "The Rhetoric of the Text: Causality, Metaphor, and Irony." *Modern Critical Interpretations: Albert Camus' The Stranger*. Ed. Harold Bloom. Philadelphia: Chelsea House Publishers, 2001. 127-138. Print.

Tisson-Braun, Micheline. "Silence and the Desert: The Flickering Vision." *Critical Essays on Albert Camus*. Ed. Bettina L. Knapp. Boston: G. K. Hall & Co., 1988. 42-56. Print.

The Changing Raskolnikov vs. Ethical Meursault

By Andrew Alonzo

Camus' *The Stranger* reflects Dostoevsky's *Crime and Punishment* in both structure and story line. In Dostoevsky's *Crime and Punishment*, the main character, Raskolnikov, is both moral and immoral. He is immoral from the beginning of the story, however by the calculated murder, that was planned. He understands his actions, however he justifies them to himself, but ends up feeling remorse for them later. In Camus' *The Stranger* the main character, Meursault, appears to be unethical and almost nihilistic, but this is an inaccurate depiction of him. In actuality, he is an ethical character that does not understand his wrongdoings. Meursault's murder is different from Raskolnikov's in that it was spontaneous and almost mechanical in nature. Meursault's innocence is proved through the fact that he does not understand his own actions or the consequences of them. Dostoevsky's Raskolnikov, like Camus' Meursault, is a moral character; however, Raskolnikov starts of as immoral and makes the transformation to moral, whereas Meursault is moral from the beginning.

Dostoevsky has had an incredibly large impact on Camus' literary work. Therefore, there is a huge comparison to be made between Dostoevsky's Raskolnikov and Camus' Meursault. Both stories have similar story lines, and both revolved around a seemingly immoral character, that when looked at closely is actually moral. At the time of his actions, Raskolnikov understands what he is doing, thus making him seem immoral. However, it is at the end of the novel that he shows his moral side. He becomes very religious because of Sonya and feels sympathy for the wrongs he has done. Dostoevsky makes it so that Raskolnikov starts of as an immoral character, but changes into a moral one by the end of the novel.

The first significant insight into Raskolnikov's lack of morality is shown in his response to his mother's letter to him. His mother writes a lengthy letter letting him know what is going on back home. Raskolnikov reads the letter and he feels bitter and angry at his sister's situation. The book states, "Almost all the time that Raskolnikov was reading this letter his face was wet with tears, but when he came to the end it was pale and convulsively distorted and a bitter angry smile played over his lips" (Dostoevsky 33). This bitter angry smile is the beginning of Raskolnikov's impending rage. However, it is important to note that despite his sister's sacrifice, at this point he is doing nothing more to help his family out. His lack of morality, and care for his family, shines through as he shows his selfish and immoral side.

The next part of *Crime and Punishment*, which truly shows Raskolnikov's lack of morality, is when he carefully plans and executes murder. The act of planning the murder is very immoral in itself. To effectively plan a murder a person has to understand what he or she is doing, and then design a way to carry out that plan. Raskolnikov, on the other hand, understands his murder plans and uses the science of nihilism to justify it. In the novel, Raskolnikov says, "One death, and a hundred lives in exchange-- why it's simple, arithmetic!" (Dostoevsky 56). It is through this comment that his rationale is seen. Raskolnikov's use of the science of nihilism to justify murdering the woman is his effort to make it a moral act. Justifying his intentions allows him to make it a moral act inside his own mind, therefore making him a moral character in his own mind. Thus, his act of planning the murder is immoral, and his quick thinking to try to justify his plan is acknowledgment of his own immorality.

Raskolnikov's science of nihilism as justification for the murder of the old lady is inaccurate. However, when looking at from a utilitarian prospective, it does make sense. She was a wealthy woman who could use her money to save a starving family. In the journal entitled *Philosophy*, Sophie Botros says, "Raskolnikov murders a rich old woman on worthy Utilitarian grounds -- she is vicious, her life is barren, and he will kill her and give her money to a large starving family" (Botros 440). This theory is quixotic in that there is no talk of Raskolnikov ever donating the money. The money is not his to give, and therefore he is unable to donate it to other people. Conversely, in Raskolnikov's mind this theory is completely valid. This makes him a moral character for wanting to the best deed for the largest number of people. His morality is short-lived.

The next scene, in which Raskolnikov acts immoral and inhumane, is when he is actually murdering the old woman. The murder itself is extremely immoral; however, it is more immoral how inhumane Raskolnikov was in the process. Rather than causing the old lady a quick death, he beat her head in with blunt end of the axe. The passage in which the murder occurs reads as follows:

> Because she was so short, the axe struck her full on the crown of the head. She cried out, but very feebly and sank into a heap on the floor, still with enough strength left to raise both hands to her head. One of them still held the 'pledge.' Then he struck her again and yet again with all his strength, always with the blunt side of the axe, and always on the crown of the head. (Dostoevsky 66).

The fact that Raskolnikov used the blunt side implies that he wanted the old lady to suffer while she died. He could have easily used a knife to slit her throat and make it a faster death and less painful. However, he chose to use the blunt end of an axe to strike her three different times. The way in which Raskolnikov murdered the old lady was very slow and very painful. This makes his act even more immoral than a normal murder because he exhibits inhumane characteristics. It is not only is his inhumanity that is a problem, but at this point in the novel he is immoral.

An instance in which Raskolnikov's immorality can be seen is when he is faced with punishment. When he realizes that he needs to be tried for the crime, he starts to understand the concept of his punishment. He starts to accept that what he did was not truly justified and that he needs to be punished for the murder. Sophie Botros makes note of this in her journal "Acceptance and Morality" when she says, "when one reads depictions as vivid and detailed as those as Raskolnikov's acceptance of imprisonment, when his moral need for punishment is brought so compellingly before us, the notion of a right to punishment ceases to seem absurd and begins to become morally plausible" (Botros 436). Botros talks about how important punishment is in the moral aspect of Raskolnikov's existence. She makes note that it important for the morals of society that Raskolnikov is punished for his crimes. However through her interpretation, one can also understand that the reason for the need of moral punishment is because of Raskolnikov's immorality.

During the second half of the novel, Raskolnikov slowly makes the change from immoral to moral. It is in this half of the novel that he accepts his own fate and decides that he needs to confess to the murder. It is also in this part of the novel that he accepts his sentence and turns himself into Porfiry. After the second half of the novel there are two epilogues in which Raskolnikov turns to religion. It is only after he turns to religion that he starts to feel remorse and guilt for the crime that he has committed.

When looking back on the murder, it becomes apparent that Raskolnikov is when the reader realizes that he only hurt himself through his crime. This leads to a lack of remorse for his crime, until the epilogue in which he becomes religion. Scholar Maurice Beebe explains this lack f remorse. He says, "The absence of remorse may be explained by not only his sense of the chain of fate that led to the murder, but also his overwhelming conviction that he is the principle victim of his crime." (Beebe 156). When analyzing Raskolnikov's actions, it Beebe's explanation is logical. The fact that Raskolnikov believes that the murder was "a chain of fate" rather than his own actions explains his lack of remorse. A person will not feel remorse for something they do not feel responsible for, especially if he believes that he is a victim of his own crime. This lack of remorse points to a moral state of mind within Raskolnikov because it shows that he feels that he has done nothing wrong. It is not until after he converts to religion that he feels sorry for what he has done.

Although the remorse does not come until the epilogue of *Crime and Punishment*, Raskolnikov has doubts about his actions. He does not know why he is doing what he is, and therefore it leads him to doubt his actions. He questions his reasoning for the murder, thus allowing the reader to see the confusion within his own mind. He says, "If it all has really been done deliberately and not idiotically, how is it I did not even glance into the purse and don't know what I had there, for which I have undergone these agonies, and have deliberately undertaken this base, filthy degrading business" (Dostoevsky 110). It is through this quote that the reader is able to understand Raskolnikov's confusion. He is truly trying to question himself about his intentions behind the murder of the old woman. He is unsure whether his action was deliberate, making him immoral and unethical, or if his action was idiotic and an "event" rather than an "act." This confusion is one of the highlights in the reason for Raskolnikov's change to a moral character by the end of the second epilogue.

It is in his confession that Raskolnikov starts to understand his wrongdoings. He realizes that he needs to confess to be punished for the crimes that he did. With the help of Sonya, he understands that he needs to confess and do the moral thing. Dostoevsky scholar George Gibian comments on this, he says, "Sonya persuades Raskolnikov not only to confess and wear the cross, but also to kiss the earth at the crossroads -- a distinctly Russian and pre-Christian acknowledgement of earth as the common mother of all men" (Gibian 991). This religious symbolism that Gibian talks about from *Crime and Punishment* is symbolic of the beginning of his change into a moral character. The symbolism starts the beginning of the change in which he starts to become part of his own life again. The religious symbolism is the beginning of his transformation to a moral character. The religion represents morals and values, which will be instilled in him once he completes his transformation to a religious person, with Sonya's help, and eventually into a moral character.

Sonya helps Raskolnikov by helping him find a religion, and also admitting to the crime. She does not force him into admitting the crime; however, she does persuade him to see the moral side of it. It is only once Raskolnikov sees the moral aspect of his murder that he feels the need to confess. Nevertheless, he is not strong enough to confess on his own. Dostoevsky Scholar, Snodgrass wrote an article entitled "Crime for Punishment: The Tenor of Part One" that talks about this. The passage reads, "Porfiry, recognizing Raskolnikov's desire for punishment, first preaches to him the need for confession, then makes that confession possible by setting an example" (Snodgrass 202). This desire of punishment that Snodgrass mentions is a symbol of Raskolnikov's realization with the crime he has committed. He understands what he has done wrong and that it is immoral, and his need to confess shows that he knows he needs to be punished for it. Through this need to confess, fully knowing he will be punished, Raskolnikov's morality is shown.

It is in the epilogue of the novel that Raskolnikov makes is transformation from immoral to moral. He does so by using religion as a guide for the right values to follow. Sonya is the main person that influences him; however, it is Raskolnikov's choice whether or not he wants to be moral. He chooses to do so. In the epilogue, when talking about the New Testament it says, "He himself had asked her for it not long before his illness and she had brought it to him without a word" (Dostoevsky 464). This was the beginning of his transformation right before he got sick. Dostoevsky goes on to say, "...an idea flashed through his mind: 'Could not her beliefs become my beliefs now?...'" (Dostoevsky 464). It is through this moment that Raskolnikov realizes that he is accepting religion as a way to become moral. He understands his wrongdoings and wants to become a better person, so he uses religion as a way to do it.

Now that Raskolnikov's transformation from immorality to morality can be seen, it is important to look at Albert Camus' version of Raskolnikov. Although Camus did not copy Dostoevsky's Raskolnikov, the main character from his book, *The Stranger*, was influenced by him. The character Meursault resembles Raskolnikov in that they both seem immoral, both commit a crime, and both are punished for it. Raskolnikov, as stated above, makes a transformation from immoral to moral. However, Meursault is very different, he does not understand his own actions, and therefore is a moral character throughout the entirety of the novel. Meursault may be initially perceived as immoral, however once one can comprehend his inability to understand his own life, it is recognizable that he is actually a moral character that does not understand the consequences of his own actions.

In the beginning of *The Stranger*, Meursault reflects back on his relationship with his recently deceased mother. Meursault is talking about how he has never had a great relationship with her. In one scene in particular, Meursault is talking with the caretaker about seeing his deceased mother in the casket. He told the caretaker that he did not want the casket to be opened so that he could see his mother. When the caretaker asked why, Meursault replied with "I don't know" (Camus 6). Although it is not abnormal for a person to decline seeing a departed relative, it is uncommon for the person to have no understanding of his or her own actions. A normal response would be "I do not want to remember her like that." This is just the beginning of the insight to Meursault's extremely confused mind. Once again, if a person is confused, and unsure why he does what he does, then it is unrealistic to say that person is immoral.

Meursault's lack of understanding of his own life is exemplified with additional evidence that he does not understand his own wrongdoings. In his article entitled "Camus and The American Novel," Harry Garvin states, "The main reason is that Meursault has an inalienable sense of his own being and individuality. Everything he feels and does has a naturalness and logic for him, but all things in the world that conflict with his being are alien to him" (196). Garvin explains Meursault's predicament. The fact that Garvin explains that things at conflict with Meursault's being are "alien to him" can be used to support the point that society's rules of morality are foreign to him. Consequently, if he does not understand the rules of society, it is not ethical to say that Meursault is immoral, and therefore, by default, he is moral.

Later, the fact that Meursault does not understand his own motivations is made more apparent. The incident in which Meursault kills the Arab is not carefully calculated like that of Raskolnikov. This incident happens purely by chance. An immoral act is not one that happens by chance, because, once again, morality is something that is conscious. Therefore, immorality is conscious. Scholar Richard Lehan in his article entitled "Camus's L'etranger and American Neo-Realism" writes:

> The point is that the murder of the Arab is as accidental and gratuitous as Camus' world itself. Meursault does not mean to kill the Arab. He goes to the spot by accident. He meets the Arab by chance. The sun happens to be unpleasantly hot, and Meursault happens to feel terribly uncomfortable. When the Arab draws a knife, the blade by chance catches the sun and the reflection flashes into Meursault's eyes whereupon he responds mechanically -- like a coiled spring -- and the gun goes off (Lehan, 234).

This quote talks about Meursault's "mechanical" action when he shoots the Arab. He shot the Arab without even thinking about it, but it was his first reaction without a conscious thought. In addition, he talks about how the whole incident was not on purpose or planned, but that it was purely based on initial reaction or "instinct." Also, as Lehan stated that Meursault meets the Arab by "chance" emphasizes the fact that the shooting was not done on purpose. Therefore, if there was no conscious act while committing murder it could not have possibly been immoral. This lack of conscious activity during a crime is the reason why the "insanity plea" exists. For that reason, the action is moral, but the person may be unsafe for society.

The insanity plea was created for people like Meursault that is unaware of his own actions. According to an article entitled

"Venirepersons's Attitudes to the Insanity Defense: Developing, Redefining and Validating a Scale," in the journal of *Law and Human Behavior*, scholars Skeem, Louden and Evans write that the insanity plea is "a defense for acquittal based on the defendant's inability to appreciate or control his actions because of mental illness or defect" (Skeem, Louden and Evans 624). Although Meursault does not have a mental illness, he does have a mental defect. He is unable to control his own actions, and therefore acts spontaneously. Thus, the reason that his actions were considered "mechanical." He was not thinking about his actions, but instead he acted off of the flash of light off the knife blade and shot the Arab multiple times.

Even more evidence that Meursault is a moral character comes when he is placed into jail. He is placed into a cell with several other Arab. The passage of *The Stranger* reads, "They laughed when they saw me. Then they asked me what I was in for. I said I'd killed an Arab and they were all silent" (Camus 72). This is significant because if Meursault realized that what he did was wrong, he would have not admitted to killing the Arab to his cellmates. Due to the fact his cellmates were Arab, Meursault should have been scared about admitting his crime. He was not afraid to admit his crime, because in his own mind, he did nothing wrong. It was the sun that caused his actions, not his own conscious actions. Therefore, it is not accurate to call Meursault's actions "immoral."

Even more evidence which supports that Meursault is a moral character, and not in control of his actions comes during the trial. The judge asks Meursault if he has anything to add to his testimony. Meursault replies "I never intended to kill the Arab" and then later he continues to tell the truth and says, "Fumbling with my words and realizing how ridiculous I sounded, I blurted out that it was because of the sun" (Camus 102). These quotes are very important to understanding Meursault's mentality. Once again, it shows his lack of understanding of his own motivations. However, it also shows his true reason for killing the Arab. In Meursault's mind, it truly was the sun that motivated him to murder the Arab. He understands how ridiculous he sounds. Nevertheless, he continues to go with the truth, that the sun caused his actions. The fact that he does not alter his defense after he understands how senseless he sounds shows that he does not truly understand everything that is going on. He does not have control of his own life, once again preventing him from being immoral.

There is more evidence to support the fact that Meursault is an honest and moral character. Garvin comments on this, "Being incorrigibly honest, Meursault makes understandable and even acceptable to us his objective feeling towards his mother, the four shots, and his reasons for acting or not acting" (Camus 196). This reference supports the idea that because of Meursault's honesty and reasoning, that his actions are seen as acceptable. The fact that Garvin uses the word "acceptable" shows that once his reasoning is understood, that Meursault is actually moral. What society considers acceptable, is what defines a moral act to that specific society, once again showing the certainty of Meursault's morality.

After the trial, Meursault is awaiting his fate in his jail cell when a priest comes to visit him. The priest tells him that he has to free himself from a sin. A sin, especially in the case of murder, would be considered an immoral act. Meursault replies by saying, "I told him I didn't know what a sin was. All they had told me was that I was guilty. I was guilty, I was paying for it and nothing more could be asked of me" (Camus 118). This is even more evidence that Meursault cannot comprehend the moral aspect of his crime. Meursault, even after his fate has been decided, continues to acknowledge that he does not understand what he did wrong. Meursault is a moral man and does not understand what he did wrong to obtain the charges against him. Therefore, it makes sense that he does not have sympathy for his wrongdoings.

Meursault has no sympathy, again because of his lack of understanding, but also because of his feeling of lack of control. The insanity plea argument that was stated before applies again here. Once again Meursault did not have control of his actions, and therefore many people see the murder as an event more than an act done by Meursault. According to scholar Gerald Morreale "Some critics insist on referring to Meursailt's act as a murder, others see it as an 'event' rather than an 'act'" (Morreale 456). The idea that it is an "event" rather than an "act" supports the insanity plea. Meursault's mechanical action supports the idea that it was more of an event rather than an act. If it was an act, Meursault would have thought about it beforehand, rather than responding with a mechanical action while firing the pistol. The mechanical action suggests that Meursault's "act" was actually an event, thus explaining why he does not understand his own actions.

By the end of the novel, it is apparent that Meursault's understanding of his life is still unclear. No matter what he does throughout the course of the novel, his actions were all driven by the moment, not by conscious thoughts. In his article entitled *Raskolnikov Through the Looking-Glass: Dostoevsky, and Camus's L'etranger*, author Sergei Hackel states "Meursault remains detached to the very end, even though society assumes control of his body and intends to kill him"(Hackel, 195). Hackel's interpretation of the story offers another perspective of the point that Meursault is unaware of the things that are going on in his life. He is not able to be sad for his own life, because he is unable to piece together that what he did is "immoral" by society's standards. However, since he does not understand it, one cannot claim that he is immoral, because morality is conscious. Hackel uses this quote from *The Stranger* to solidify his point about Meursault: "All that remained to hope was that on the day of my execution there should be a huge crowd of spectators and that they should greet me with howls of execration" (122). This highlights Hackel's point, and shows what Meursault looks forward to. He looks forward to the hateful feelings from other people. Through this quote his morality shines through. The fact that Meursault is not scared of people, but that he looks forward to their hate, emphasizes that he does not truly understand what is going on.

When analyzing the morality, or lack thereof, it is important to understand that Dostoevsky influenced Camus. Therefore, Raskolnikov and Meursault have striking similarities, but they are not exactly alike. They both have seemingly moral and immoral characteristics. However it is Raskolnikov, who influenced Meursault, which makes a transformation from immoral to moral. Meursault on the other hand, is a moral character from the start. However Camus makes Meursault seem immoral, which makes him seem like Raskolnikov. It is only when one takes a close look into the personalities of the two characters that they realize that one undergoes a transformation, and the other was moral to begin with, but seems immoral due to his lack of understanding of his own life. Dostoevsky's influence on Camus shows through the similarities between Raskolnikov and Meursault.

Bibliography

Beebe, Maurice. "The Three Motives of Raskolnikov: A Reinterpretation of Crime and Punishment." *College English.* 17.3 (1955): 151-158. National Council of Teachers of English. Web. 24 May 2010.

Botros, Sophie. "Acceptance and Morality." *Philosophy.* 58.226 (1983): 433-453. Cambridge University Press. Web. 24 May 2010.

Camus, Albert. *The Stranger* trans. and ed. Matthew Ward. Vintage Books: New York, NY. 1988. Print.

Dostoevsky, Feodor. *Crime and Punishment* trans. and ed. George Gibian. WW Norton: New York, NY. 1989. Print.

Garvin, Harry. "Camus and the American Novel." *Comparative Literature.* 8.3 (1956): 194-204. Duke University Press. Web. 25 April 2010.

Gibian, George. "Traditional Symbolism in Crime and Punishment." *PMLA.* 70.5 (1955): 979-996. Modern Language Association. Web. 23 May 2010.

Hackel, Sergei. "Raskolnikov through the Looking-Glass: Dostoevsky and Camus' 'L'Etranger.'" *Comparative Literature.* 9.2 (1968): 189-209. University of Wisconsin Press. Web. 24 April 2010.

Lehan, Richard. "Camus's L'etranger and American Neo-Realism." *Books Abroad.* 38.3 (1964): 233-238. University of Oklahoma. Web. 24 April 2010.

Morreale, Gerald. "Meursault's Absurd Act." *The French Review.* 40.4 (1967): 456-462. American Associationg of teachers of French. Web. 26 May 2010.

Skeem, Jennifer., Louden, Jennifer., and Evans, Jennee. "Venirepersons's Attitudes toward the Insanity Defense: Developing, Refining, and Validating a Scale." *Law and Human Behavior.* 28.6 (2004): 623-648. Springer. Web. 26 May 2010.

Snodgrass, W.D. "Crime for Punishment: The Tenor of Part One." *The Hudson Review.* 13.2 (1960): 202-253. The Hudson Review Inc. Web. 24 May 2010.

Eternity: Loneliness and Self-Isolation

By Iosif Todoran

In a world where life is perceived by many to be without purpose, hope or meaning, there remains an unprecedented idea of the meaning of life. A century ago scholars attempted to illustrate this by provoking the idea on nihilism through literary genius. They offered a channel to access the despair of existence. Two scholars: Fyodor Dostoevsky, a Russian novelist, and Albert Camus, a French thinker, wrote thought provoking novels such as, *Notes From Underground* and *The Stranger,* which examined the philosophy of nihilism. The protagonists in each of the novels, Underground Man and Meursault, illustrate this philosophy in action. Underground Man and Meursault are two unethical men who view life as meaningless and whose immoral actions consequently drive them to isolation. Furthermore, their behavior towards those around them, especially women, exudes their inner demons, in turn, sealing their fate of an eternity of loneliness and self isolation.

Dostoevsky's novel, *Notes From Underground*, displays a protagonist named Underground Man whose life is centered in nineteenth-century St. Petersburg Russia, precisely in the 1860s. Underground Man is a minor civil servant who has completely alienated and isolated himself from society, who has never experienced love, and as a result turned into a bitter man who finds life to be meaningless. He describes himself as sick, spiteful, and he believes his consciousness to be overdeveloped. Dostoevsky reveals to the reader a glimpse of the mind of a man tormented by his own self-isolation. Furthermore, he has become delusional in his own philosophy. Dostoevsky's focal point of the novel lies within Underground Man's beliefs. Moreover, his self-loathing and ill will cripples him, and consequently leads him to a life of loneliness and complete isolation. To illustrate, Underground Man's spends his days as a civil servant making petitioners miserable. One day, he meets Liza, a 20 year old prostitute who left her parents and came out to St. Petersburg for a better life. His inexperience with love causes him to push Liza away, losing the only possible source of love he could have had in his life.

The Stranger is a narrative that describes the protagonist named Meursault, whose lack of emotion detaches him from the people in his life, and ultimately leads him to a life of isolation. His reaction to life throughout the novel illuminates the lack of intimate relationships he has with others. His self-isolation from those around him distances him from his emotions, positive or negative; furthermore, his physical and sexual behaviors are his only outlets. He maintains emotionless relationships throughout the novel, such as his neighbor, Raymond, and his girlfriends Marie; however, none are as or more important than his relationship with Marie. He is infatuated with her and the constant need for sexual release portrays him as a sensualist who acts solely on his physical desires. Marie professes her love for Meursault, only to consequently add volume to his indifference to all things around him. In addition, after his mother's death and the murder of an Arab, he shows no feelings of love, regret, remorse or sadness; and his actions reflect his indifference and careless attitude towards the world.

Notes from Underground and *The Stranger* are two novels which deal with similar issues pertaining to nihilism. According to *The New Dictionary of the History of Ideas,* nihilism is total and absolute destructiveness, and the ideology that life has no intrinsic meaning or value (Cassedy). A nihilist believes in nothing and has no purpose in life except an impulse to destroy and cause crisis. Doubt, disbelief and destructive attitudes are an extreme form of nihilism where individuals such as Underground Man and Meursault see the world as a tool of destruction, along with the lack of these values, morals and lack of accountability for their actions they find ways justify these behaviors. Even though the novels are written almost a century apart, they portray two different, yet very similar protagonist characters, whose lives are parallel in many ways and their views on life are identical. Both Underground Man and Meursault do not value life, instead they view life as pointless with no intrinsic value or meaning. Underground's nihilistic view on life not only further isolates him but rather shapes his character into a bitter, malicious, vengeful man.

Underground man states, "I was a nasty official. I was rude and took pleasure in it. When petitioners used to approach my desk for information, I'd gnash my teeth and feel unending pleasure if I succeeded in causing someone distress. I almost always succeeded" (Dostoevsky 3). Underground man's heart is filled with bitterness towards all aspects of society and inasmuch, as he is aware that he is powerless to act against it or within it; he uses his civil servant position to cause petitioners before him turmoil. He is an unethical, malicious man, who abuses his power by condescending petitioners, in turn feeding his inner demon, through the misery of others. Furthermore, his irrational aggression towards the petitioners consequently fuels his inner demon, which in turn magnifies his self constructed loneliness until he finally reaches complete isolation.

Underground Man's isolation from society and dissatisfaction with his solitary life drives him into a state of extreme obsession where he spends enormous amounts of time plotting revenge. One night as Underground man passes by a little tavern, he notices some gentlemen fighting with billiard cues. He enters the tavern, and an officer walks by him, grabs him by the shoulders and moves him to the side, leaving Underground Man with an empty feeling; thus, unleashing a choler river of obsession with the officer. He is determined to retaliate against the officer, by not acknowledging him. Underground Man states, "Afterward I used to meet this officer frequently on the street and I observed him very carefully. I stared at him with malice and hatred, and continued to do so for several years! My malice increased and became stronger over time" (Dostoevsky 35). Underground Man, consumed by his rage towards the officer, spends several years of his life stalking him and waiting for the perfect opportunity to retaliate. Underground Man's immoral and irrational actions have no objective, because no sane gentleman spends several years plotting revenge for no apparent reason on an officer they do not even know. Furthermore, no ethical well-respected gentleman stalks another and hates him for years for simply moving him to the side. Underground Man's isolation not only causes him to lose his mind and disregard all things in the real world as he focuses solely on his avenge on the officer, however at the same time he takes his bitterness out on those around him, such as his servant Apollon.

Underground Man mistreats Apollon by not paying him his wages on time and takes advantage of the fact that he is his master. Underground Man says, "I was so embittered by everyone that I decided, heaven knows why or for what reason, to punish Apollon by not paying him his wages for two whole weeks" (Dostoevsky 80). Apollon, an innocent bystander, falls prey to Underground Man's nihilistic existence. For no reason at all, he holds an honest man's salary, who works hard for his wages, just because he feels like it. Underground has no regards for anyone else's well being and due to his misery; he feels the need to make everyone else around him miserable. His unethical behavior towards Apollon consequently unleashes his dark side, which in turn completely detaches him from all people around him and brings him a step closer to eternal loneliness.

His loneliness briefly falters one night as he encounters Liza, who has the potential to grow to love him. However, his bitter cold heart inflicts emotional pain decreasing his chances for potential love. Liza is a young, naive woman who has no family around and sells her body to make a living; she is a lost soul waiting for a hero. Underground Man takes advantage of the situation and attempts to convince her there is a better life out there. However, he fails miserably. The nihilism that governs his life clouds his true reasoning for wanting to help her and instead he brings her to tears. Underground Man speaks "...suddenly [she] burst forth cries and moans. Then she pressed her face even deeper into the pillow: she did not want anyone, not one living soul, to hear her anguish and her tears. She bit the pillow; she bit her hand until it bled" (Dostoevsky 73). Due to his lack of experience with love, Underground Man's inability to show tenderness and care towards Liza causes her to burst into tears, as a result of his condescending words towards her. He plays with her feelings and as soon as she stops crying, he hands her his address and invites her over to his house, Liza accepts.

Underground Man's lack of ability to love throughout his life brought him to the point of pushing away the only person in his life who has the ability to love him back unconditionally. After days of daydreaming about Liza coming to visit him, and how he would be her hero rescuing her from her days of misery, the moment finally comes. Liza shows up at his door steps and tells him how much she wants to get away from the place she is in. It is as if she was crying out to him, longing for his love and rescue. Instead of comforting Liza, he mistreats her, belittles and makes her burst out into tears once again. Underground Man begins to speak "I cursed you like nothing on earth on account of that address. I hated you already because I'd lied to you then, because it was all playing with words, dreaming in my own mind. But, do you know what I really want now? For you to get lost that's what!" (Dostoevsky 85). Through these harsh words Underground Man breaks Liza's heart. She came to see him according to his invitation, instead of a hero, she found a heartless unethical man whose inner demon exudes words that inflict pain consequently creating wounds difficult to heal. His unethical behavior towards Liza predetermines his eternal fate of loneliness by distancing her away from him in turn causing him further isolation from the whole world.

Underground Man's self-isolation and detachment from those around him drives him to his fate of eternal loneliness. Similarly to Underground Man in *Notes From Underground*, Meursault's nihilistic view on life in *The Stranger*, and unethical actions towards those around him in turn seals the same fate, this being an eternity of loneliness. In addition, Meursault uses his emotional detachment and self-isolation as a coping mechanism to deal with the meaningless of his self-imposed nihilistic existence. In the same way as Underground Man's unethical and immoral actions are ubiquitous in all of his relationships, Meursault's unethical and immoral behavior is prevalent in all his relationships. He sees meaninglessness in the entire world around him and also in the people closest to him, because of the nihilism that presides over his life.

Meursault is portrayed as a detached, unemotional and an amoral man who is deprived of human feelings and whose apathy knows no bounds. According to, *The American Heritage Dictionary*, "an amoral person is someone who lacks moral sensibility and does not care about right or wrong" (Amoral 60). Meursault's interactions with those around him exemplify his careless attitude about what is right or wrong, causing him to isolate himself as he does not express much feelings in relationships or during emotional times and views his life as pointless, not taking into consideration the consequences to follow. He takes things in life as they come, and nothing really matters to him. Meursault thinks that everything he has done in life truly signifies nothing, and all he can account for is what he is experiencing in the present moment. When life is over, existence is also over, and the hope of some sort of salvation is pointless. Meursault finds the meaning of existence to be pointless, as he displays passiveness and through his lack of emotion towards the people and events described in the novel.

His emotional non-responsiveness to the news of his mother's death is the first of Meursault's sign of immoral behavior and self-imprisonment that he brings upon himself. His only escape is to be emotionally detached, because that is the only way he can deal with the meaningless and self-isolation he bounds himself to. Meursault says, "Maman died today. Or maybe yesterday maybe, I don't know. I got a telegram from the home: 'Mother deceased. Funeral tomorrow. Faithfully yours.' That doesn't mean anything. Maybe it was yesterday" (Camus 3). He is indifferent to his own mother's death, that he has no idea when she died. In addition, any man who is so emotionally detached from his own mother to the point of carelessness is not considered moral. Meursault's lack of sympathy to his mother's death is apathetically disturbing. He recounts the dubious facts of his mother's death, as plainly as the telegram had stated it. His first reaction to his mother's death is not sadness it is a matter-of-fact unemotional acceptance of the situation. When Meursault attends the funeral, he complains more about the sun rather than showing remorse for his own mother, and he does not show any outward signs of grief. Furthermore, the lack of emotion at the funeral and his disturbing detachment exudes his inner demon and consequently leaves him vulnerable which drives him to complete isolation from the world around him; in turn, adding volumes to the self-isolation and loneliness.

His immorality furthermore surfaces, through his actions, in the relationship, with his neighbor Raymond, who is a violent abusive man that beats his girlfriend. He calls Meursault into his room to tell his tales of violence and to seek advice from him. During their conversation, Meursault remains quiet. However he eventually speaks up. Meursault has not only emotionally detached himself from his own mother, but also from any future relationships. He views them as meaningless, consequently causing him to further display immorality through his actions. Meursault states, "Marie said it was terrible and I didn't say anything. She asked me to go find a policeman, but I told her I didn't like cops" (Camus 36). Due to his self-isolation and inability to feel compassion for anyone, Meursault takes no action to calling the police. Therefore, his immorality overpowers him as he does not act. Meursault's indifference towards calling a police officer or feeling any kind of remorse for the incident demonstrates that Meursault is incapable of showing the least concern even when someone is being hurt. This further displays his nihilistic view that all things in life are meaningless and there is no intrinsic meaning or value to anything. Due to his nihilism and immorality, Meursault sees no point in getting involved in Raymond's abusive behavior towards his girlfriend.

Meursault is apathetic in all his relationships thus far, and just as Liza is the only capable love for Underground Man, similarly, Marie is the only woman in Meursault's life capable of loving him. Meursault says, "A minute later she asked me if I loved her. I told her it didn't mean anything but that I didn't think so. She looked sad" (Camus 35). Marie asks Meursault if he loves her and bluntly says he does not think so because he is somewhat afraid that if he were to say he loves her then that would mean that he cares and he is not as nihilistic as he portrays himself to be. Meursault's incapability of expressing any kind of feeling towards Marie is called Inexpressive Male Syndrome. According to Sociology professor, Linda Rillorta, Inexpressive Male Syndrome is a term used for "males who are unable to express their feelings" (Inexpressive Male Syndrome). Meursault is unable to express the way he feels about Marie, because to him it all means nothing and none of it matters. The emotional detachment from his mother foreshadows his emotional detachment to Marie. Later, Marie proposes marriage to Meursault and again his indifference causes Marie sadness. A moral man expresses his true feelings for the woman he loves, but Meursault's immorality and self-isolation cripples his ability to do so. His display of apathy towards Marie only further reveals that his focus is mainly on the physical fulfillment rather than the emotional aspect of their relationship, which in the end only adds to his self-constructed loneliness.

Meursault's self-isolation and loneliness drives him to the point where he shoots the Arab in cold blood. He kills the Arab instantly with the first shot. He does not cease fire but rather takes his frustration that has been accumulating through his insignificant relationships and the world out on the Arab. Meursault states, "Then I fired four more times at the motionless body where the bullets lodged without leaving a trace. And it was like knocking four quick times on the door of unhappiness" (Camus 59). With each shot he takes at the motionless body, there is a release of energy, and the pressure he is under is alleviated. In comparison one can describe it as a "mental orgasm" similarly as the orgasm achieved with Marie physically, with the exception that it was simply in his mind where his self-imposed nihilism began (Francev 1AH). Meursault's firing four more times is his release of the mental frustration of his self-imposed nihilistic existence that has been expanding since the beginning of the novel; consequently, driving him into the brink of his immorality where he ends up punished by death through execution. Furthermore, his actions exude his inner demon that not only drives him to complete loneliness but also to complete isolation from the world.

Underground Man and Meursault are very similar in the way they both end up: miserable, lonely and with no one to love them. Their nihilistic view on life cripples their ability to learn how to love. In turn they live a life of loneliness and isolation with bitterness and un-fulfillment. Due to the lack of family love and affection in their lives, they both end up losing their only chance of experiencing love. Underground Man pushes Liza away through his cruel and hurtful words and Meursault drives Marie away through his indifference and inability to express love and affection.

Meursault's and Underground Man's nihilistic view of life, unethical and immoral actions towards those around them, consequently drive them to complete isolation. This in turn, fuels their inner demons, exuding their loneliness, which in turn seals their fate of an eternity in complete isolation. Underground Man's nihilistic state of being drives him to complete loneliness and isolation from those around him. He abuses his civil servant position to make his petitioners miserable. He becomes obsessed with the officer for not acknowledging him at the bar and spends several years plotting revenge. In addition, he pushes away Liza, the only woman in his life capable of showing him love. Relatively to Underground Man, Meursault isolates himself from the world, shows no emotion at his mother's funeral or compassion when Raymond beats up his girlfriend. He pushes Marie away, with his inability to show emotion when she professes her love for him. Seeing that they are both nihilistic the question of ethics and morals are irrelevant, because one can either be nihilistic or moral but not both. If Underground Man is to meet Meursault, they would agree on the meaninglessness of life, and their paths would coincide and form parallel nihilism.

Bibliography

Camus, Albert. *The Stranger*. New York: Random House, Inc., 1989. Print.

Cassedy, Steven. "Nihilism." *New Dictionary of the History of Ideas*. Ed. Maryanne Cline Horowitz. Vol. 4. Detroit: Charles Scribner's Sons, 2005. 1638-1641. *Gale Virtual Reference* Library. Web. 26 Apr. 2010.

Dostoevsky Fyodor. *Notes From Undergound*. Michael R. Katz New York: W.W. Norton and Company, Inc. 1989. Print.

Francev, Peter. "Lecture on *The Stranger*" 14 April 2010.

"Amoral" *The American Heritage Dictionary of the English language*. Fourth edition. 2000. Print.

"Inexpressive Male Syndrome" Rillorta Dr. Linda. Sociology. *"Lecture on Males"* 4 April 2010

"But deliver us from Evil": God, Man and Evil in Albert Camus

By Giovanni Gaetani

Introduction

In a note of his Notebooks, dated 1st November 1954, Albert Camus expresses as following his reluctance to the label of «atheist» that often some critics gave him: «I often read that I am atheist, I often hear talking about my atheism. But these words mean nothing to me, they have no sense for me. I do not believe in God and I am not atheist». In the last conjunction «and» - that appears in cursive - a big and unresolved problematic is concentrated : is Camus atheist, and if not, what are the reasons of this answer? How is possible to not believe in God and, at the same time, to consider himself not atheist? Are we just talking about a sort of agnosticism or about something different and more complex? The aim of our work is to answer to all these questions: subdividing Camus' work in four different but strictly connected periods, we will analyse the evolution of the relationship between Man, God and Evil, in order to define without any prejudice or misunderstanding the position of Camus' philosophy concerning God's problem.

As regards our subdivision of Camus' work - but also our theme in general - we have two references. The first one is a note from the fourth notebook (January 1942 - September 1945), named Without tomorrow:

> What do I meditate bigger than me, and what do I feel without being able to define it? A sort of difficult march towards a sanctity of negation, an heroism without God, the pure man then. All the human virtues, including the loneliness in front of God. [...] My work will have as many forms as the stages in the road of a perfection without reward. The stranger is the zero point. Idem the Myth. The plague is a progress, not from zero to infinite, but towards a deeper complexity that still has to be defined. The

finishing line will be the saint, but he will have an arithmetic value, measurable as the man.

The second reference, that clearly legitimate our subdivision, is a personal explanation from Camus himself, released in occasion of the Nobel prize withdrawal and quoted by Roger Grenier in his introduction to the Camus' complete works:

> I had an exact plan when I started my work: I wanted first of all to express the negation. Under three forms. Fictional: and it was The stranger. Dramatic: Caligula, The misunderstanding. Ideological: The myth of Sisyphus. I foresaw also the positive under three forms. Fictional: The plague. Dramatic: State of Siege and The Just. Ideological: The rebel. I saw yet a third blanket of this plane in the theme of love.

At this point, our journey in the Camus' universe can start. As already mentioned, our first stage will be the so called «Mediterraneanity».

The man between world's harmony and God's absence: the Mediterraneanity

In the preface to his early text The Wrong Side and the Right Side (1937), Albert Camus speaks about an «injustice of climate» whose he was «for long time, without knowing, a profiteer». He is talking about his fortune to be born in a country where «the sea and the sun are free»: this country is Algeria. There our author had the opportunity to look at the world under a special light that disclosed just the pleasant and harmonic part of reality. Let us consider that: a person born in a cold and grey country, where nature constantly show his hard and pitiless face, surely would have a particular consideration of life itself. He would think that world is not an hospitable place, where men have not to fight to live: for him, life will be strictly connected with strain and pain. We are not saying that this person should be sadder than one's born in a friendly and warm land: we are just affirming that their points of view on life would be very different.

Albert Camus has one of this rare and special point of view on life: although he was born in a poor and unlucky family - his father died in the first world war when he had just one year, his mother was deaf and stammering from the childhood for an accident - and although since seventeen he suffered tuberculosis, he had always the opportunity to live his «everlasting summer» under his «invincible sun». This harmony and this brightness is reflected and transposed by Camus in his first texts. Yet their titles are meaningful for us: Nuptial, Summer - but also what he calls Solar Essays - all these expressions indicate the Mediterraneanity. Let us try to define it: it is the original condition where man lives in harmony with the world, in a natural balance where light dominates and no «shadows of thought» fall. So it is on the one hand a pre-reflexive and pre-conceptual condition, on the other hand a full-silence and solitary one: here man lives almost as an animal, immersed in his sensitivity and sensuousness, far from the «thought's tragedy» in which soon he will find himself.

In this condition, man appears to be free from any constraint and suffering: nothing seems to threat him and what nature gives him is enough to live. For this reason, he is at the moment miraculously free from evil and - even more miraculous fact - from God itself: in fact, since nature reveals just its beneficial face, there is no reason to claim God. Yet from now we can make a rough draft of what after will be our central formula: no evil, no God. An excerpt from Nuptials at Tipasa (1939) suggest that:

> Those who need myths are indeed poor. Here the gods serve as beds or resting places as the day races across the sky. I describe and say: "This is red, this blue, this green. This is the sea, the mountain, the flowers." Need I mention Dionysus to say that I love to crush mastic bulbs under my nose?

The «gentle indifference of the world» and the Evil's coming: the Strangeness

But this almost idyllic condition cannot last too much: sooner or later things will change and man will experience the cruel and indifferent face of the world. In this way, he will soon find himself «thrown in the existence» and he will recognize the real character of life: the strangeness. Some «limit situations» - using a Jaspersian term - can lead him to this new awareness: in these, the previous natural balance between man and world vanishes; the silence that was reigning inside and outside the man's soul is now interrupted by an upsetting event; man is no more at his own home, he is now a stranger in a no more familiar and hospitable world.

The aforesaid «limit situations» that lead to strangeness can be infinite, but essentially they can be classified in two groups. In the first one we find all those situations where nature show its terrifying and superhuman face - and so all those natural catastrophes like earthquakes, inundation, etc. where man is simply passive and undefended. In the second group instead there are all those situations where man find himself foreign to his own acts - acts of madness, of anger, of desperation, but also simply some mechanical gestures. Camus' work is full of examples of these two upsetting event's groups: for reason of time, we will stop just on two main references.

The first one is an early text of Camus, Wind at Djemila. In this short essay is perfectly represented the passage from the mediterranean condition to the strangeness. In the following extract, we have underlined the most significant expressions that refer to the first condition:

> There are places where the mind dies so that a truth which is its very denial may be born. When I went to Djemila, there was wind and sun, but that is another story. What must be said first of all is that an heavy, unbroken silence reigned there - something like a perfectly balanced pair of scales. The cry of birds, the soft sound of a three-hole flute, goats trampling, murmurs from the sky were just so many sounds added to the silence and desolation. [...] And one would stand there, absorbed, confronted with stones and silence, as the day moved on and the mountains grew purple surging upward. But the wind blows across the plateau of Djemila. In the great confusion of wind and sun that mixes light into the ruins, in the silence and solitude of this dead city, something is forged that gives man the measure of his identity.

As we can see, the word «silence» returns four times in this short extract. It is not just a case. The mediterranean condition itself is silent: the natural elements that here show their beauty are dumb, and so man has no interlocutor. Everything seems to be calm and imperturbable. «But the wind blows across the plateau of Djemila» and everything changes:

> I felt myself bending by the wind like the mast of a ship. Emptied inside, with the burning eyes and the chapped lips, my skin dries up to be no longer mine. Before, with the skin, I was deciphering the writing of the world. The world was tracing the signs of its tenderness or of its anger, warming up it with the summer breeze or biting it with frost teeth. But so long rubber by the wind, shaken more than one hour, dazed by the resistance, I lost consciousness of the drawing that my body was tracing.

The previous natural harmony is now torn: at this point, man recognizes that this balance was just a contingent situation, a miraculous but fleeting condition in the existence's chaos. The world itself - far from being totally friendly or, on the contrary, totally unfriendly - is simply indifferent to the human expectations and lamentations. Every values that man finds in the world is just an human projecting in an inhuman reality. An extract from The Myth of Sisyphus suggest that idea:

> A step lower (from the Absurd, Author's note) and strangeness creeps in: perceiving that the world is "dense," sensing to what degree a stone is foreign and irreducible to us, with what intensity nature or a landscape can negate us. At the heart of all beauty lies something inhuman, and these hills, the softness of the sky, the outline of these trees at this very minute lose the illusory meaning with which we had clothed them, henceforth more remote than a lost paradise. The primitive hostility of the world rises up to face us across millennia, for a second we cease to understand it because for centuries we have understood in it solely the images and designs that we had attributed to it beforehand, because henceforth we lack the power to make use of that artifice. The world evades us because it becomes itself again. That stage scenery masked by habit becomes again what it is.

Man recognizes his distance and his strangeness to the reality in which he lives. But, in a second moment, he will unfortunately recognize also his strangeness to men's world and even to himself. This passage is perfectly represented by Meursault, the protagonist of the novel The Stranger (1942) - we could also refer to other Camus' works like The Misunderstanding or Caligula, but for reasons of time that will be not possible. Meursault is a modest employer that lives alone his silent and repetitive life: he has a girl that he «probably does not love», no friends and his mother is dead just at the opening of the novel. In particular, this last fact really seems to be indifferent to him, as we can recognize reading the start of the novel:

> Maman died today. Or yesterday maybe, I don't know. I got a telegram from the home: «Mother deceased. Funeral tomorrow. Faithfully yours». That doesn't mean anything. Maybe it was yesterday.

This represents for us the strangeness of Meursault to men's world. He never acts and thinks as the society's standards suggest: he does not cry at his mother's funeral; he passes silent and alone at the balcony an entire Sunday afternoon, just watching the other persons walking; when his neighbour Raimondo tells him twice that «he is a pal», he just answer with an insignificant «yes»; when he will be accused of murder, he will not try at all to defend himself. That all because - as Camus himself said - «Meursault does not play the game»: he is outside the society's convention that forces everyone to act as in a big comedy, where everyone has his part and everyone acknowledges the same values; he is totally indifferent to this fake world and he is not able to lie. One of his most frequent and significant answer is «it does not make any difference to me» («cela m'était égal»), as in the following important extract:

> That evening Marie came by to see me and asked me if I wanted to marry her. I said it didn't make any difference to me and that we could if she wanted to. Then she wanted to know if I loved her. I answered the same way I had the last time, that it didn't mean anything but that I probably didn't love her. «So why marry me, then?» she said. I explained to her that it didn't really matter and that if she wanted to, we could get married. Besides, she was the one who was doing the asking and all I was saying was yes. Then she pointed out that marriage was a serious thing. I said, «No».

Meursault lives in that silent passivity for the whole first part of the book, until an upsetting event comes to change everything: the murder of the Arab. Meursault was with Raimondo, his wife and Maria on the beach when he decided to go to the cool spring behind the rock in order to refresh himself. There he founds the Arab, with whose he and Raimondo fought before. He wanted to avoid another fight and so to get back, but a natural strength - maybe the sunlight in the eyes, or the waves' sound, or the irritating sweat on the eyebrows - forced him to move forward. Then the irreparable happened: the Arab, seeing him moving one step forward, took a knife from his pocket; Meursault took the revolver in his hand and shot him. Five shoots, and the surreal silence in which he was living for the whole first part of the book is irremediably interrupted.

> The trigger gave; I felt the smooth underside of the butt; and there, in that noise, sharp and deafening at the same time, is where all started. I shook off the sweat and sun. I knew that I had shattered the harmony of the day, the exceptional silence of beach where I'd been happy. Then I fired four more times at the motionless body where the bullets lodged without leaving a trace. And it was like knocking four quick times on the door of unhappiness.

It is not Meursault that shoots five times, but someone else inside him. He knew constantly what was necessary to do - to get back and go away - but he could not do anything to stop himself. Here is the itself strangeness: our action are not always decided by ourself; that is a part of us that is not controlled by us.

At this point, man is confused and dispersed in a nihilistic situation: neither nature, nor men can be helpful for him. So exposed to Evil, finally «opened to the gentle indifference of the world», the God's alternative starts to be a real possibility, but it is for now rejected with a wild and furious scream - the reference is to the last words of Meursault against the priest. Only after, when the subject will be treated from a philosophical point of view, we will know exactly the reasons of this refusal - that is just what we are going to do in the next chapter, talking of the Absurd.

The Absurd

At this point, we can get to the heart of our main subject - the relationship between God, Evil and Man - because finally the three terms of the discussion are clearly disposed in front of us. Let us see then step by step what is the way that leads to the definition of absurd and so to the God's one. One of the precondition of the Absurd is the Strangeness - as already easy to guess. In order to explain better the connection between these two concepts it is important to quote another important passage from The Myth of Sisyphus:

It happens that the stage-sets collapse. Rising, tram, four hours in the office or factory, meal, tram, four hours of work, meal, sleep and Monday, Tuesday, Wednesday, Thursday, Friday and Saturday, according to the same rhythm - this path is easily followed most of the time. But one day the "why" arises and everything begins in that weariness tinged with amazement. "Begins" - this is important. Weariness comes at the end of the acts of a mechanical life, but at the same time it inaugurates the impulse of consciousness. It awakens consciousness and provokes what follows. What follows is the gradual return into the chain or it is the definitive awakening. At the end of the awakening comes, in time, the consequence: suicide or recovery. [...] There is nothing original about these remarks. But they are obvious; that is enough for a while, during a sketchy reconnaissance in the origins of the absurd.

Here is announced the supreme passage from unconsciousness to consciousness, without whose the absurd cannot exist at all. But there is another very important precondition of the Absurd that in The Myth of Sisyphus has large space: it is a fundamental desire that Camus calls with more then one name - «insistence upon familiarity», «appetite for clarity», «nostalgia for unity», «appetite for the absolute».

The mind's deepest desire, even in its most elaborate operations, parallels man's unconscious feelings in the face of his universe: it is an insistence upon familiarity, an appetite for clarity. Understanding the world for a men is reducing it to the human, stamping it with this seal. The cat's universe is not the universe of the ant-hill. The truism "All thought is anthropomorphic" has no other meaning. Likewise the mind that aims to understand reality can consider itself satisfied only by reducing it to terms of thought. If man realized that the universe like him can love and suffer, he would be reconciled. If thought discovered in the shimmering mirrors of phenomena eternal relations capable of summing them up and summing themselves up in a single principle, then would be seen an intellectual joy of which the myth of the blessed would be but a ridiculous imitation. That nostalgia for unity, that appetite for the absolute illustrates the essential impulse for the human drama.

This desire elevates us from the animal condition: while an animal has no other worry but to (out)live, man wants desperately to know the reason of his living. As Dostoevskij said: «the secret of man's being is not only to live but to have something to live for. Without a stable conception of the object of life, man would not consent to go on living, and would rather destroy himself than remain on earth». Camus explain this difference between man and animals as follows: «If I were a tree among trees, a cat among animals, this life would have a meaning or rather this problem would not arise, for I should belong to this world. I should be this world to which I am now opposed by my whole consciousness and my whole insistence upon familiarity». But at the same time this desire has a dramatic and insuperable aspect: it is impossible to be satisfied. In this perpetual tension between the man's appeal and the world's silence, in this unreconcilable contrast between the human will of a sense and the world's indifference and unreasonableness lives the Absurd:

> What then is that incalculable feeling that deprives the mind of the sleep necessary to life? A world that can be explained even with bad reasons is a familiar world. But, on the other hand, in a universe suddenly divested of illusions and lights, man feels an alien, a stranger. His exile is without remedy since he is deprived of the memory of a lost home or the hope of a promise land. This divorce between man and his life, the actor and his setting, is properly the feeling of absurdity.

For centuries man has not been aware of that absurd condition, and so he strained desperately to succeed in this enterprise: science, metaphysic and religion are the result of this millenarian strain. One by one Camus reveals the illusoriness of all these attempts to constitute the world as a unity. Let us see the motives of this illusoriness, starting from science. There is an important passage from The Myth of Sisyphus that we quote entirely:

> All the knowledge (science, in the original text) on earth will give me nothing to assure me that this world is mine. You describe it to me and in my thirst for knowledge I admit that they are true. You take apart its mechanism and my hope increases. At the final stage you teach me that this wondrous and multi-coloured universe can be reduced to the atom and that the atom itself can be reduced to the electron. All this is good and I wait for you to continue. But you tell me of an invisible planetary system in which electrons gravitate around a nucleus. You explain this world to me with an image. I realize then that you have been reduced to poetry: I shall never know. Have I the time to become indignant? You have already

changed theories. So that science that was to teach me everything ends up in a hypothesis, that lucidity founders in metaphor, that uncertainty is resolved in a work of art.

Science, that always considered its theories as the only possible truth, is instead only a descriptive faculty that can show how events happen but not why they happen. What about religion and theology? The argument is more complex, so let us proceed schematically. Maybe unexpected, both religion and theology (from now just religion) seem to start from an absurd observation: this world - in itself - has no sense and reason - by itself - cannot do anything to give a sense to the world. Up to now, nothing seems to move away from the «absurd reasoning». Nevertheless we know how from equal premises it is possible to arrive to different conclusions. That is the case we are discussing. In fact, the religion's next step is to affirm that while this world has no sense, there is another meaningful one beyond that (what Nietzsche calls an Uberwelt). This over-world justifies the first one and it is its only possible sense. But there is a main problem: the way to recognize this transcendent world is unfortunately irrational (or, as the medieval philosopher said, supra-rational) and so the man who really wants to find this world's sense must renounce to his reason in order to enter in a new dimension - the faith. What we have just said is well concentrated in the following extract, in which Camus compares the absurd reasoning with the reasoning of a fervent believer, Leon Chestov:

> To Chestov reason is useless but there is something beyond reason. To an absurd mind reason is useless and there is nothing beyond reason.

From this affirmation on, the two positions will be irremediably unreconcilable: starting from the same premise, they depart towards two opposite directions. Here we are going to describe this strident opposition. While a religious man wander from what is real and worldly - because, as already said, his reason of life is in the afterlife - the absurd man essentially decides to keep to the evidences and to the facts that he meets. The first supreme evidence is the following one: world is essentially chaotic. The second one is that nothing can be done to go beyond this chaos, even if our desire to do this is desperate:

I hold certain facts from which I cannot separate. What I know, what is certain, what I cannot deny, what I cannot reject - this is what counts. I can negate everything of that part of me that lives on vague nostalgias, except this desire for unity, this longing to solve, this need for clarity and cohesion. I can refute everything in this world surrounding me that offends or enraptures me, except this chaos, this sovereign chance and this divine equivalence which springs from anarchy. I don't know whether this world has a meaning that transcends it. But I know that I do not know that meaning and that it is impossible for me just to know it. What can a meaning outside my condition mean to me? I can understand only in human terms. What I touch, what resists me - that is what I understand. And these two certainties - my appetite for the absolute and for unity and reasonable principle - I also know that I cannot reconcile them. What other truth can I admit without lying, without bringing in a hope I lack, which means nothing within the limits of my condition?

The limits of the human knowledge are signed by the reason: narrow as they are, the man who wants to keep to the evidences must not pass this bounds - what Camus calls «Absurd walls». Instead, the man who wants to believe in God cannot avoid to go beyond these walls - with what Camus calls a «mortal leap». So, since now it appears clear that reason and faith are irremediably opposite: an absurd man prefers to understand just the few things that reason can explain; a believer instead understands everything just tracing it back to God's omnipotence - actually putting himself in the hands of the mystery; for an absurd man is legitimate to leave some questions unanswered; for a believer every question must find its answer at once. Two extracts from The myth of Sisyphus can help us:

> Our appetite for understanding, our nostalgia for the absolute are explicable only in so far, precisely, as we can understand and explain many things. It is useless to negate the reason absolutely. It has its order in which it is efficacious. It is properly that of human experience.

> That transcends, as the saying goes, the human scale; therefore it must be superhuman. But this "therefore" is superfluous. There is no logical certainty here. There is no experimental probability here. All I can say is that, in fact, that transcends my scale. If I do not draw a negation from it, at least I do not want to found anything on the incomprehensible. I want to know whether I can live with what I know and with that alone. I am told again that here the

intelligence must sacrifice its pride and the reason bow down. But if I recognize the limits of the reason, I do not therefore negate it, recognizing its relative powers. I merely want to remain in this middle path where the intelligence can remain clear. If that is its pride, I see no sufficient reason for giving up it.

It concerns a problem of honesty: the believer appeals to hope and illusion, just because he is to desperate to remain lucid in front of the absurd; his truth in unverifiable because it lives in a unreachable future, in a just-promised eternity; it accepts to suffer today because tomorrow, in the afterlife, he will be delivered from evil. The absurd man is on the opposite side: he negates the hope because he knows that it is a «fatal evasion»; he believes just in what is verifiable and he appeals just to his reason to discern between truth and falsity; last, he never accepts the evil that he suffers because he knows that it is irremediably unjustified.

My reasoning want to be faithful to the evidence that aroused it. That evidence is the absurd. It is that divorce between the mind that desires an the world that disappoints, my nostalgia for unity, this fragmented universe and the contradiction that binds them together. Kierkegaard suppresses my nostalgia and Husserl gathers together that universe. That is not what I was expecting. It was a matter of living and thinking with those dislocations, of knowing whether one had to accept or refuse. There can be no question of masking the evidence, of suppressing the absurd by denying one of the terms of its equation. It is essential to know whether one can live with it or whether, on the other hand, logic commands one to die of it.

In these words is clearly concentrated the absurd lucidity. On the other side, we know that the believer's illusion most of the times is inevitable. Both a rationalist as Husserl and a irrationalist as Kierkegaard arrives to the same conclusion: they jump. The motives of their jump does not matter at all, because what really matters is the jump itself: «Reason and the irrational lead to the same preaching. In truth the way matters but little; the will to arrive suffices. The abstract philosopher and the religious philosopher start out from the same disorder and support each other in the same anxiety. But the essential is to explain. Nostalgia is stronger here than knowledge».

The absurd man does not believe in God for a question of honesty: that is everything we can say. The rebel, instead, has some other motives that legitimate his God's refuse. In the following last chapter we are going to see these motives, that more than the others represent the Camus' position.

The revolt

At the end of our course, God appears clearly in front us as an idea born from the human unity's need. God is not something that precedes man: he has not created the world and the man; he is instead an human remedy. Until man did not face with evil, this idea was unnecessary. But suddenly the existence shows his pitiless and senseless face, and so man needs to find a urgent remedy. He cannot stand in this condition, so exposed to events that hurt and kill him: he needs a reason to suffer and to die. This idea is God itself. Camus' revolt refuses that desperate way out, because it recognizes just one evidence in the world: the evil existence and persistence. While the religious position leads to an acceptance of the suffering, the revolt instead cannot accept that unnatural attitude: it just prefers to fight against evil, without any philosophical or religious formula that avoids the struggle. In the Bernard Rieux words,

> Since the order of the world is governed by death, perhaps it is better for God that we should not believe in Him and struggle with all our strength against death, without raising our eyes to heaven and to His silence.

The rebel refuses to know whether God exists or not: some questions of this importance can remain unanswered. In fact, both the existence and the non-existence of God would not compensate the God's absence from the world and the evil's insurmountable persistence in the world: men - atheists or believers - are all equally distant from the God's dumb indifference. In this common distant and solitude they can gather together in name of something that does not transcends their condition and their knowledge's boundaries: the revolt.

The revolt is not a question of anger, neither of blasphemy: it is instead a question of lucidity and responsibility. Caligula said with a nihilistic tone: «Men die and they are not happy». The rebel answers that we must face with this truth. When Tarrou remembers to Rieux the temporariness of all his victories, he answers that this is not a good reason to stop from going on. So described, the revolt can seem to be a particular kind of humanism, but that is not true, because the rebel has not the same hope and the same optimism on man that an humanist had: he is instead aware of the animal side of the man, and he knows that any ideal man's definition is useless (or harmful) when not connected with reality. But at the same time the rebel's position is not simply an agnosticism, which concludes with an epochè on God's existence just using logic argumentations. The revolt is all of that and more: it is a lucid look on reality full of courage and brightness that answer to God's absence with his persistent and valiant responsibility.

Bibliography

Albert Camus:

The Stranger, Vintage International, New York 1989;

The Myth of Sisyphus, Penguin, London 2000;

The Rebel, Penguin, London 2000;

The Plague, Vintage International, New York 1991;

Notebooks 1935-1951, Marlowe & Company, New York 1998;

Notebooks 1951-1959, Ivan R. Dee Publisher, Lanham 2008.

Understanding Albert Camus' Absurd as Ambivalence, and its Relevance for Existential and Psychodynamic Approaches

Matthew H. Bowker

Introduction: Contemporary Ambivalences

Over the past thirty years, increasing numbers of researchers in political and social scientific fields have argued that uni-valent, one-dimensional models of human attitudes are inadequate to describe the complexity of human experience. Social psychological investigations of ambivalence have been applied to a wide range of topics, from parenthood to race relations, from the selection of presidential candidates to attitudes about abortion and the death penalty. For over a century, psychoanalysts have argued that ambivalence, in various shapes and guises, is at the heart of psychological life. It might even be argued that ambivalence (although not always going by that name) has been treated as a central aspect of the human condition since Goethe, Pascal, Montaigne, Shakespeare, even Attic tragedians and the authors of the wisdom books of the Tanakh.

Sociologists, anthropologists, and historians like Robert Merton (1976), Clifford Geertz (1968), and Robert Jay Lifton have all argued that the ambivalent demands made by contemporary cultural norms and political institutions require a more dynamic understanding of the relationship between self and society, as individuals seem to struggle with incongruities in their environments and the "absurdity" implied by "the absence of 'fit'... between individual self and outside world" (Lifton 1993, 94). The era of late modernity, or "high modernity," as Anthony Giddens (1991) calls it, is often described as an era not only of particularly rapid change, but of increasingly contradictory and ambivalent pressures, of a "push and pull... mix and break," that operates on levels from the global to the personal (Chan and

McIntyre 2001, 4). If Roland Robertson's (1995) term, "glocalization," expresses some of the ambivalences at work in some contemporary societies, Stephen Castles (1998) has outlined them more fully by highlighting several "fundamental contradictions" at the heart of global change, including the contradictions between "inclusion and exclusion," "the Net and the self," "modernity and post-modernity," and the "national and the global citizen."

In only slightly different terms, Giddens' well-known *Modernity and Self-Identity* describes the psychological impact of a world full of increasingly intense 'dilemmas'. These dilemmas are of an ambivalent nature: "unification versus fragmentation," "powerlessness versus appropriation," "authority versus uncertainty," "personalized versus commodified experience," and ontological security versus existential anxiety (1991, 181-208). Giddens argues that increasingly 'reflexive selves' must strive to heal the terrible rifts in their experience occasioned by these dilemmas, beneath which lies a constant and "looming threat of personal meaninglessness" (1991, 201).

However we characterize the challenges of the twentieth and twenty-first centuries, large-scale social change is increasingly recognized as something that penetrates "through to the very grounds of individual activity and the constitution of the self" (Giddens 1991, 184). As advances in communication technologies increase exposure to difference, contradiction, and crisis, often making the latter "a normal part of life" (Giddens 1991, 184), Kenneth Gergen has argued that we are witnessing the advent of "multiphrenia," which is "the splitting of the self into a multiplicity of self-investments" (2000, 73-74). For Gergen, the "social saturation" brought on by frequent but discontinuous contact with an increasing number of others, of options, and of possibilities causes a sort of over-population of the self, where we exceed even Walt Whitman in containing greater and greater 'multitudes', to the detriment of our values and relationships (Gergen 2000, 68-80).

While the psychoanalytic understanding of the term 'ambivalence' still guides contemporary usage, a number of recent studies and applications of the concept, such as those mentioned above, have dislodged it from a purely psychoanalytic context. For instance, the philosopher Philip Koch uses the term 'ambivalence' to refer to all kinds of "conflicted feelings" (1987, 258n). Likewise, Ihor Zielyk's taxonomy of ambiguity and ambivalence defines ambivalence as "the taking of a mixed stance toward a social object or category of objects" (1966, 57). Steve Harrist, in his interesting phenomenological investigation of ambivalence, takes ambivalence "in the broadest sense," meaning simply "attraction and/or aversion... so as not to prematurely restrict the horizon of inquiry" (2006, 87). Harrist construes ambivalence to mean "both sides are strong" or "both sides have their own worth" (2006, 91); his interviews begin with the simple question: "Can you describe a time when you had more than one feeling?" (2006, 94).

A psychodynamically-informed but broad definition of ambivalence as conflicting emotions serves us best in attempting to clarify the meaning of Camus' absurd. Such a definition respects the etymology of the term as dual (*ambi*) emotional forces (*valences*) while distinguishing it from 'ambiguity', which denotes indeterminacy or uncertainty. It also follows standard usage: "A duality of opposed emotions, attitudes, thoughts or motivations, which a person simultaneously holds towards a person or object, is the centerpiece of the standard psychoanalytically shaped definition of ambivalence" (*Oxford English Dictionary* 1989). More importantly, this definition permits us to make use of the psychodynamically-informed understanding of 'ambivalence' as it was established by Eugen Bleuler and Sigmund Freud in the early 1900s and later developed by Melanie Klein and others.

This paper argues that a fruitful analogy may be drawn between the philosophy of the absurd and the concept of ambivalence. It is important to clarify, however, that it is not necessary to *reduce* Camus' idea of absurdity to any of the more traditional psychoanalytic categories of ambivalence, e.g., ambivalence about mothers, ambivalence resulting from the Oedipus conflict, or ambivalent sexual or destructive drives. Instead, I seek to use our understanding of the dynamics of ambivalence, an understanding that has been informed by psychoanalytic and social scientific study, to explore very similar properties of Camus' concept of the absurd. I try to use ambivalence as an *analogy* to explicate the absurd, primarily by applying the mechanics of ambivalence, if you will, to the emotional material of the absurd. In the first section of the paper, I briefly review relevant approaches to ambivalence, in order to lay a foundation for the analogy with the absurd that follows.

A Brief History of the Concept of Ambivalence

Eugen Bleuler, a contemporary of Sigmund Freud, used the term 'ambivalence' in his *The Theory of Schizophrenic Negativism* (first published in 1910), but it is his *Dementia Praecox or the Group of Schizophrenias* (completed in 1908 but not published until 1911) that is widely credited as the first comprehensive psychoanalytic investigation of ambivalence (Graubert and Miller 1957, 458; Harrist 2006, 87; Lorenz-Meyer 2001, 3-4). In both of these works, Bleuler defined ambivalence as the simultaneous presence of contradictory thoughts, feelings, or volitions. As such, he found ambivalence to be present in 'healthy' and 'normal' individuals as well as in those whom he diagnosed with *dementia praecox*, or precocious dementia, otherwise known as schizophrenia.

Bleuler characterizes ambivalence as both a universal and potentially pathological phenomenon.

> Even for the healthy everything has its two sides. The rose has its thorns. But in ninety-nine out of a hundred instances, the normal person compares the two aspects, subtracts the negative from the positive values. He appreciates the rose despite its thorns. The schizophrenic, with his weakened associative linkings does not necessarily bring the different aspects of a problem together. He loves the rose because of its beauty and hates it because of its thorns... Certainly even under normal conditions, synthesis may be omitted. The healthy, too, feels something like 'two souls in his breast'; and he, too, would be less inclined to speak so much of sin if it did not also have some pleasant connotations. (1950, 374-375)

The difference between ambivalence among 'healthy' individuals and 'sick' ones, therefore, was not precisely the presence of ambivalence, but rather the ability to hold it together, to sustain a consistent view of an object in spite of its ambivalent appraisals. Whereas the 'healthy' individual came to accept his or her ambivalence as a mixed stance toward an object, the schizophrenic in Bleuler's theory was forced either to oscillate between all-good and all-bad impressions, or to split the object in two, one loved and one hated.

Bibliography

Albert Camus, *Between Yes and No*, Albert Camus: Lyrical and Critical Essays (Vintage 1970)

Albert Camus, *Caligula*, Albert Camus: Caligula and other plays (Penguin 2006)

Albert Camus, *Cross Purpose*, Albert Camus: Caligula and other plays (Penguin 2006)

Albert Camus, *The Outsider* (Penguin 1982)

Albert Camus, *The Rebel* (Penguin 2000)

Bleuler reminds us that, while certain expressions of, defenses against, and responses to ambivalence may be taken as a sign of illness, no one is exempt from ambivalence or from the pressures that it generates. Rather, Bleuler finds ambivalence at work even in ordinary life. Just as his patient tries to escape a locked ward moments after telling him (with what appears to be sincerity) that he has no further interest in escaping, when Bleuler enters a large store, he confesses that "I wish to get something at a particular counter; I carefully determine the one I do not wish to go to, but then it is that very one to which I go" (1950, 375).

While Bleuler applied 'ambivalence' broadly, in reference to any number of conflicting ideas, emotions, beliefs, affects, and volitions, Freud would narrow its reference but afford it an even greater significance. While it is not incorrect to say that Freud's operating definition of ambivalence was "the co-existence of [love and hate] simultaneously directed towards the same object" (Freud in Graubert and Miller 1957, 460), such a definition understates and over-specifies the profound ambivalences and conflicts that inform almost all of Freud's thought: ambivalences not only about love and hate, but about pleasure and pain, survival and the self, life and death. Freud's use of the concept of ambivalence is commonly traced to his *A Phobia in a Five-Year Old Boy* (1909), better known as the case of Little Hans, although ambivalence plays a role in earlier works like *The Interpretation of Dreams* (1900) as well as Breuer's and Freud's *Studies on Hysteria* (1895), where Freud saw the origin of psychoneurotic symptoms in the repression of traumatic "incompatible ideas" (Greenberg and Mitchell 1983, 27, 33).

In the short section of *The Interpretation of Dreams* rather fittingly devoted to *"Absurd Dreams,"* Freud argues that dreams regularly reflect emotional conflict and that dreams of a dead loved one, for instance, are marked by an "especially profound ambivalence of feeling which controls the relation of the dreamer to the dead person" (1900, 295-296). Freud notes that it is common in such dreams for the deceased person to alternate, as it were, between being dead and alive; and he interprets this as a fantasized indifference. The purpose of this fantasized indifference, Freud explains, "is to help the dreamer to deny his very intense and often contradictory emotional attitudes, and so it becomes the dream-representation of his *ambivalence*" (1900, 296, emphasis in original). Here, dreamed indifference protects against ambivalent feelings, feelings that are especially intolerable when concerning a deceased loved one. Of course, Freud would return to many of these ideas and relate them to loss, identification, and melancholy in *Mourning and Melancholia* (1917, 250-251, 256-258).

For Freud, ambivalence is at the root of neurosis but it is not exactly its efficient cause. Rather, ambivalence, which is universal, is exaggerated and exacerbated to different degrees by different individual reactions to it. Freud understood neuroses as attempts to cope with ambivalence "while effectively preserving it and restraining behaviour" (Lorenz-Meyer 2001, 4), and in *The Dynamics of Transference* (1912) and *The Unconscious* (1915b), depicted the unconscious as a 'reservoir', a 'seething cauldron' for those intolerably intense or persistent ambivalences which must be held down by the organized personality (see Giovacchini 1982, 12)

While hatred remains in the unconscious, defensively intense conscious feelings of love must counteract them, contributing to a greater ambivalent conflict within the individual. This process of repressing one feeling and exaggerating its opposite compose part of Freud's concept of reaction-formation, elaborated in his later *Inhibitions, Symptoms, and Anxiety* (1925). With the cooperation of the unconscious, ambivalence can therefore divide ambivalent feelings, paralyze the will, or displace ambivalent conflict over any number of everyday matters. The compulsive individual, for instance, repeats his protective measures in order to compensate for the growing doubts he has displaced from his ambivalent love and hatred onto his memory, his observations, his intentions, and even the reliability of the physical world (Freud 1963, 74-77).

In *Repression* (1915) and the *Introductory Lectures* (1916-1917), Freud describes the incomplete or ineffective neutralization of ambivalence which permits the child or patient suffering from neurosis to ignore ambivalences that would otherwise generate conflict in the adult because of the development and unification of the adult personality (Graubert and Miller 1957, 460-461). In fact, Freud argued that the persistence of unreconciled ambivalent attitudes was apparent not only in children and patients but in groups and in so-called 'primitive societies' (see Freud 1959, 15-16n; Graubert and Miller 1957, 459). The "primordial ambivalence" at the root of Freud's concept of guilt in *Civilization and its Discontents*, for instance, is an about the conflicts at the root of collective life (1961, 94-95).

Throughout his various treatments of ambivalence, Freud is clear that conflict is a part of normal psychic life. And although we are not always consciously aware of our ambivalence (indeed, *because* we are not), we should not forget that "emotional life... is in general made up of pairs of contraries" (Freud 1909, 113). It is at least partly because Freud viewed the human experience as one of ambivalence, one in which our mental life is "perpetually agitated by conflicts which we have to settle" (Freud in Abel 1989, 39), that he often insisted that there was no clear line between neurosis and normality, that "an unbroken chain bridges the gap between the neuroses in all their manifestations and normality" (Abel 1989, xv).

Melanie Klein, by her own accounts a Freudian, but whose work diverged from Freud's in several ways (see Alford 1989, 23-26; Greenberg and Mitchell 1983, 120-121; Minsky 1998, 33), posited basic ambivalences at the heart of the psychological life of the child. For Klein, "the central conflict in human experience... is between love and hate, between the caring preservation and the malicious destruction of others" (Greenberg and Mitchell 1983, 142). One might say that, for Klein, we are ambivalent at birth, experiencing almost immediately a conflict between life and death instincts (see Segal 1964, 12-13). Even before children face conflicting desires and restrictions, Klein thinks ambivalence confronts infants who fear not reprisals from parents, but the consequences of aggression and the projections of their own anger and rage. Basic ambivalences exist, she argues, even at a very young age, between experiences of comfort and frustration, between feelings of love and gratitude and feelings of envy, anger, and fear.

Klein finds that the earliest and most radical solution to the presence of ambivalent feelings is to split the world, the parent, or even the self into two categories, absolutely good and absolutely bad. The goal of splitting is "to keep persecutory and ideal objects as far as possible from one another, while keeping both of them under control" (Segal 1964, 13-14). Splitting is a reaction to ambivalence in the sense that it seeks to prevent conflicting feelings from coming into contact with each other, so that the bad does not destroy the good. Thus, bad and good are separated and exaggerated, making both poles increasingly extreme. In the struggle to contend with ambivalent experience in both a loving and an anxiety-ridden environment, splitting is, at first, a *necessary* defense for the developing child. Splitting, like ambivalence itself, may serve first as a healthy protection against overwhelming threats to the self. But, if severe splitting continues, it becomes a regressive defense that precludes further development.

It is only after a certain security has been attained that ambivalence, which, itself, is "partly a safeguard against one's own hate and against the hated and terrifying objects," may gradually decrease (Klein 1975, 350). Successful tolerance and integration of ambivalence means that the child is able to see significant others as real persons, just as successive non-threatening experiences in reality permit the child to tolerate greater and greater degrees of ambivalence. The resulting 'depressive position' is the result of the gradual abandonment of radical splitting and the gradual integration of the good and the bad into whole people and a whole self, both of which may contain good and bad qualities.

The depressive position is therefore the announcement of a more mature, more moral, and more creative position: one in which the child seeks to manage his or her ambivalence, feels a growing responsibility, desires to make reparations to others, and constructs a more integrated identity on proto-moral grounds (see Minsky 1998, 41). Indeed, "the pain of mourning experienced in the depressive position, and the reparative drives developed to restore the loved internal and external objects, are the basis of creativity and sublimation... to recreate and to create" in the name of care, reparation, and preservation of the good (Segal 1964, 62).

Thus, in Klein's theory, ambivalence is, itself, ambivalent. The agonal forces that increase the child's anxiety eventually permit the child to enter and work though (although never completely) the challenges of the depressive position. And the splitting reactions to them are at first developmentally adaptive, then regressive and destructive. Although Klein wrote almost exclusively of children, she thought that continued splitting "under the stress of ambivalence to some extent persists throughout life" (Klein 1975b, 75n), arguing even that "we have an example of this [splitting of imagos] in the phantastic belief in a God who would assist in the perpetration of every sort of atrocity (as lately as in the recent war) in order to destroy the enemy and his country" (Klein 1975, 203n). Her approach suggests that, with maturity, it is possible to contend with ambivalence through the gradual the discovery of moral and creative resources in the personality.

While we should not overlook the dangers and limitations of psychiatric approaches, the concept of ambivalence is very closely related not only to the clinical work of Klein, but to what appears to be an increasingly prevalent set of behaviors and experiences known as the borderline personality. Almost all theorists of borderline personality emphasize that it presents with dis-integrated, contrary, or conflicting affects and behaviors. The typical symptoms of emotional lability and dis-integrated personality are thought to be rooted in a defense against unbearable conflict, in the taking of an extreme posture to protect the self from the terrifying threats of 'bad' self- and object-representations (see Kernberg 1975, 5-7; Kernberg 1984, 12-13; Cooper and Arnow 1984). Recent interpersonal theories have also argued that borderline symptoms suggest the presence of heightened psychological conflict (Benjamin 1993; Kiesler 1996), and a recent empirical study revealed that individuals with borderline diagnoses evinced a higher degree of ambivalence and inconsistency with respect to self-assessments of warmth, dominance, and other qualities (Hopwood and Morey 2007). This recent theory and research suggests that a non-integrated emotional conflict or ambivalence may be at the root of the constellation of affects and behaviors now most often classified as borderline.

Otto Kernberg emphasized the borderline tendency to revert to primary-process thinking and to rely on primitive defenses like splitting, denial, early forms of projection, projective identification, omnipotence, and devaluation (Kernberg 1984, 15-17). Splitting, as we have discussed, means essentially to deny ambivalence, conflict, or contradiction by dividing the world into separate and extreme categories of 'all good' and 'all bad'. The borderline personality tends to undertake and maintain such splits in order to protect itself from dangerous aspects of the self and others, in order to preserve a tenuous hold on the 'good'. Since the notion of giving up the split threatens to contaminate the 'good' with the 'bad', we may say that the borderline personality splits in order to avoid a kind of ambivalence, to avoid a situation in which good and bad might co-exist in the self or in others.

Unfortunately, splitting is not only a result of a threatened or defensive self, but can be a cause of continued anxiety and instability. That is, the reversion to this type of defense against ambivalence does not help the individual develop the capacity to tolerate ambivalence or to integrate conflicting emotions or experiences. Rather, as Kernberg points out, "a vicious circle is created by which ego weakness and splitting reinforce each other" (Kernberg 1975, 29). This vicious circle manifests itself in continued splitting and dis-integration, as well as rapidly changing affects and emotions, radical shifts in thoughts and feelings about the self and others, and "sudden and complete reversals of all feelings and conceptualizations" about the self or others (Kernberg 1975, 29).

Integration of ambivalent or contradictory perceptions of others is made especially difficult due to the "constant projection of 'all bad' self and object images [which] perpetuates a world of dangerous, threatening objects, against which the 'all good' self images are used defensively, and megalomanic ideal self images are built up" (Kernberg 1975, 36). That is, although borderline defenses are attempts to protect the self by splitting the world into impossible contraries, they perpetuate an experience of life in which the precarious and ephemeral 'good' inside is constantly threatened from both within and without. The fact that the borderline personality deals in such excessively abstract, extreme, and unreal images further precludes any realistic assessment and understanding of self and others, which perhaps only reinforces the tendency toward interpersonal emotional shallowness and paranoia (Kernberg 1975, 166-167). Thus, the tendency to split, to radically idealize, and to radically devalue makes any rapprochement with a stable social reality increasingly problematic.

As I hope to show now, both ambivalence and splitting are extremely important themes in Camus' reflections on the absurd. Sometimes Camus' own protests, such as "I want everything explained to me or nothing" (1955, 27), rely on a kind of splitting, an insistence on all or nothing. But, more often, Camus' thought on the morality of the absurd is an argument *against* the dangerous consequences of splitting the world into absolute good and absolute evil. Camus' absurd person, as we shall see, lives with profound ambivalences about losing him/herself in an 'all', asserting him/herself against a 'nothing', and affirming, rejecting, or remaining indifferent to good and evil. But Camus seeks to articulate and interpret these dangers (albeit without using psychological language) in order to avoid the facile solution of splitting the world and the self into absolute good and bad.

In spite of these connections, it is imperative that we not confuse the absurd, itself, with the borderline personality, or any other specific psychiatric category. For the purposes of this paper, I loosely refer to splits and related defenses as reactions to a kind of ambivalence, inasmuch as they defend the self against the threats and anxieties created by the mixing of highly-charged contraries. And yet, as we shall see, no particular defensive reaction exhausts the *many* possible responses one may have to ambivalence or to the absurd, nor is it the case that one must be suffering from any illness other than being human to experience such ambivalences. Camus will address the desire to be indifferent and the desire to be committed, to be univocal and to be silent, to be perfectly separate and to be inextricably linked, to be natural and to be intellectual, along with many other ambivalent emotions, none of which accord perfectly with any single psychoanalytic theory, but all of which may be informed by a broad understanding of the human dynamics of ambivalence.

Camus' Ambivalent Absurd

John Cruickshank finds that basic antagonisms run from Camus' early *Noces* through *The Myth of Sisyphus*: "*Le Mythe de Sisyphe* sharpens the dualism of *Noces* to such an extent that this dualism takes on all the discordancy of a paradox. Now it is clear that one can live less easily with a paradox than with a dualism" (1960, 46). By distinguishing between dualism and paradox, Cruickshank alludes to one of the central dilemmas facing the absurd: the difficulty of living with it. This difficulty, he explains, and the "recognition of a paradox, together with persistent thinking about it, gives to *Le Mythe de Sisyphe* some sort of double tension so that the book opens on a note of anxious inquiry" (Cruickshank 1960, 46). This double tension, this anxious inquiry, I argue, is comprehensible only in the context of the dynamic of ambivalence set out above.

For Camus, absurdity is the tension between two sets of powerful desires. Some of Camus' most memorable passages are his descriptions of a deeply-felt desire for unity, for clarity, for wholeness. At times, this desire is expressed in terms of a longing for transcendent meaning and values, or for the passion and intensity that absolute beliefs and principles would permit. At other times, it is expressed in naturalistic or romantic imagery, as a fusion with the world, an immersion in water, a merger with a landscape or climate. On the other hand, Camus also effectively conveys a profound revulsion for this ideal of merger or unity. He offers memorable denouncements of the consolations of certainty, God, eternal truths, 'leaps of faith', and absolute values, repudiating overly-reconciled actions as a kind of rationalized crime. Camus often makes dramatic refusals of unity and wholeness in favor of the realities of suffering, revolt, and exile. He disparages 'escapes', along with anything that smacks of the inhuman or the superhuman, on the grounds that they do violence to the self and to individual experience.

In this section of the paper, I briefly examine these two general categories, the desire for and the rejection of unity, as the constituent elements of an ambivalent absurd position. Understanding the absurd in this way dramatically changes its most traditional interpretations as meaninglessness, evil, or the brutality of nature. Absurdity is perhaps related to these notions, but, at best, they only represent *parts* of its ambivalent composition. If we must speak about the absurd in terms of meaning, evil, and nature, I propose that we learn to speak of the absurd as comprising *both* terms (good and evil, meaning and meaninglessness, nature and humanity) along with the complex tensions between them. For Camus, I hope to make clear that the most relevant ambivalence is between unity and individuality, wholeness and independence, selflessness and the self.

The Desire for Unity

Camus is at his most passionate when he describes what may be called his desire for unity, for clarity, for wholeness. But, as with other areas of his thought, Camus describes this desire in a daunting variety of ways. He refers to it as the "desire for unity" (1955, 51), a "wild longing for clarity" (21), an "insistence upon familiarity" (17), a "longing to solve" (51), an "appetite for the absolute" (17, 51), a "longing for happiness and reason" (28), a "nostalgia for unity" (17, 50), and an "impulse that endlessly pursues its form" (1956b, 262).

One thing that unites these various expressions of the desire for unity is that Camus presents them all as essentially human, irreducible, and undeniable. Camus persuades us of the presence of this desire, but he does not speculate about any deeper biological, psychological, or spiritual origins. "The mind's deepest desire," Camus writes, "even in its most elaborate operations, parallels man's unconscious feeling in the face of his universe: it is an insistence upon familiarity, an appetite for clarity" (1955, 17). Camus claims that our profound desire for unity is the primary psychological force shaping human life: "That nostalgia for unity, that appetite for the absolute illustrates the essential impulse of the human drama" (1955, 17).

In ways that continue to inspire comparisons to Pascal, Camus persuades us that the knowledge of eternal or absolute principles would provide us with a kind of intellectual beatitude. "If thought discovered in the shimmering mirrors of phenomena eternal relations capable of summing them up and summing themselves up in a single principle, then would be seen an intellectual joy of which the myth of the blessed would be but a ridiculous imitation" (1955, 17). In fact, "all would be saved," Camus writes, "if one could only say just once: 'This is clear'" (1955, 27). With language that seems intended to evoke themes of enlightenment, Camus describes the experience of being "divested of illusions and lights" (1955, 6), lost in darkness, outside of the familiar, and disconnected from ourselves and others. In this murky and mystified condition, we see no past and no future, we are "deprived of the memory of a lost home" just as we are denied "the hope of a promised land" (1955, 6).

But in responding to this desperate situation, we see that the drive for intellectual clarity really expresses a deeper desire for unity. The real object of Camus' demand for explanations and reasons is to become one with the world. In one case, it is the fantasy of a world with human properties that permits a feeling of identity: "If man realized that the universe like him can love and suffer, he would be reconciled" (Camus 1955, 17). In another case, this craving for identity requires a self-dehumanization, so as to become elemental and thus identical with the natural world: "If I were a tree among trees, a cat among animals, this life would have a meaning, or rather this problem would not arise, for I should belong to this world. I should *be* this world" (Camus 1955, 51, emphasis in original). Both of these visions of identity suggest that the joy of clarity, to which Camus compared the myth of the blessed, may really be a joy of oneness, a joy of living in a world without difference, and perhaps, a joy of living without the demands of individuation.

In a slight variation, Camus' describes the longing for clarity in a way not entirely dissimilar to the critique of reason offered by Frankfurt theorists. "Understanding the world for a man is reducing it to the human, stamping it with his seal... The truism 'All thought is anthropomorphic' has no other meaning. Likewise, the mind that aims to understand reality can consider itself satisfied only by reducing it to terms of thought" (1955, 17). Here, Camus speaks explicitly about 'reducing' and deforming phenomena by 'stamping' them into images of himself, molding them to fit his intellectual categories. These manipulations allow the individual to master, to grasp, to comprehend what he encounters. Thus, the longing for clarity is presented not only as a longing for unity and non-difference, but as a desire for control and possession.

Whether one craves clarity, identity, or control, the desire for unity appears throughout Camus' early work as both an intellectual demand and an emotional impulse. By the time he writes *The Rebel*, Camus has not clarified the nature of this desire, calling it variously an idea, a passion, and a demand for form, reconciliation, and finality. What is clear, however, is the fact that the desire for unity remains unsatisfied, which only serves to heighten absurd ambivalence and tension. Camus explains:

> [Life] is only an impulse that endlessly pursues its form without ever finding it. Man, tortured by this, tries in vain to find the form that will impose certain limits between which he can be king. If only one single living thing had definite form, he would be reconciled!... Appearance and action, the dandy and the revolutionary, all demand unity in order to exist, and in order to exist on this earth... It is not sufficient to live, there must be a destiny that does not have to wait for death. It is therefore justifiable to say that man has an idea of a better world than this. But better does not mean different, it means unified. This passion which lifts the mind above the commonplaces of a dispersed world, from which it nevertheless cannot free itself, is the passion for unity... Religion or crime, every human endeavor in fact, finally obeys this unreasonable desire and claims to give life a form it does not have. (1956b, 262)

The Desire for Selfhood

While Camus convincingly describes the power of our desire for unity, he simultaneously argues that the fulfillment of this desire is both impossible and repugnant. It is difficult to find an appropriate name for this desire that contrasts so sharply with the 'desire for unity'. A kind of *principium individuationis*, one would like to call it the desire for 'self-preservation', but the connotations of that term in the sense of *physically surviving* are a bit too strong for Camus' subtler concerns. Camus wishes to preserve the intellect, the memory, and a kind of personal relationship to these things that can only be characterized as a 'desire for selfhood', a desire to preserve individuality and experience accompanied by a rejection of the loss of self implied by the desire for unity.

Camus claims that the existential philosophies he reviews in *The Myth of Sisyphus*, without exception, "suggest escape" (1955, 32). They suggest escape from the very dilemma they set out to solve, by "deify[ing] what crushes them and find[ing] reason to hope in what impoverishes them" (1955, 32). But from what, exactly, do these philosophers seek escape and why, exactly, should they not? The answers to these questions form the content of the second half of the ambivalence of the absurd.

Perhaps Camus' most famous rejection of unity is his demand "to live solely with what he knows, to accommodate himself to what is, to bring in nothing that is not certain... to find out if it is possible to live *without appeal*" (1955, 53, emphasis in original). In spite of our desire for unity, he writes, "we fall into the ridiculous contradiction of a mind that asserts total unity and proves by its very assertion its own difference and the diversity it claimed to resolve" (1955, 18).

Reason fails us in our attempts to unify experience. In fact, it begins to deny experience when it refuses to acknowledge that one of the few things of which we feel certain is our own, simple, unreasonable existence. "This heart within me I can feel," Camus writes, "and I judge that it exists. This world I can touch, and I likewise judge that it exists. There ends all my knowledge, and the rest is construction. For if I try to seize this self of which I feel sure, if I try to define it and to summarize it, it is nothing but water slipping through my fingers... Between the certainty I have of my existence and the content I try to give to that assurance, the gap will never be filled" (1955, 19).

Faced with this contradiction, this gap, the absurd individual is thrust back upon himself. He comes to realize that he will never find the clarity and unity he seeks, that he will never "apprehend the world" (1955, 20). Yet this is not an easy discovery for Camus; rather, it represents a devastating insult, a terrible defeat, for "there is no happiness if I cannot know" (1955, 21). If we fail to find the reasonable, clear understanding we seek, Camus argues that this failure does *not* suggest that we should negate the desire for unity that prompted our quest. Instead, Camus claims that we can "negate everything of that part of [us] that lives on vague nostalgias, except this desire for unity, this longing to solve, this need for clarity and cohesion" (Camus 1955, 51).

Camus' assertions about matters of knowledge, doubt, certainty, and the reality of sensory and emotional experience have annoyed certain philosophical critics. But, to be fair, Camus is not interested in speculating about the reliability or verifiability of senses, emotions, or perceptions. Nor is he, as some have thought, defending a Cartesian method or advancing a skeptical philosophy. Rather, Camus seems to be trying to describe, in unfortunately abstract and philosophical terms, the ambivalence of absurdity. Camus is claiming that, in spite of himself, he is unwilling to discredit his experience. He feels unwilling to forget the limits, boundaries, and flaws in his fantastic desires. He is unwilling to escape his *"raison dérisoire"* (1955, 51), which, rather than "ridiculous reason," might be better translated as 'ridiculing reason' or 'derisive reason' because it mocks our hopes and fantasies. This ridiculing reason stubbornly refuses to be carried away by wishes for unity or wholeness, setting the absurd person in opposition to himself. This condition in which one is opposed to oneself, torn between desires, caught between feelings of integrity and estrangement, is one of profound ambivalence, which, perhaps understandably, feels very much like being set "in opposition to all creation" (1955, 51).

Many critics have mistaken Camus' absurd because Camus, himself, often either pretended or mistakenly believed that his investigation of absurdity was guided by a commitment to pure logic and methodical reasoning. Camus pretends to dedicate himself to a rigorous "method" in both *The Myth of Sisyphus* and *The Rebel* (1955, 11, 30). Throughout the opening essay of *The Myth of Sisyphus*, for example, Camus proclaims that he will conduct his pursuit "without reckless passion, in the sole light of evidence" (1955, 9), maintaining the "lucidity imposed on [him] by the pursuit of a science" (1955, 21). He uses language like "evidence" (1955, 6), "logic" (1955, 9), and "data" (1955, 30-31), as if there were a scientific method at work in his speculations about the absurd.

But even casual readers should notice that Camus' insistence upon logic and rationality is not based upon a sober commitment to objectivity or a disinterested analysis of his subject. There is not, in *The Myth of Sisyphus or The Rebel,* a reasoned or grounded defense of a skeptical method, or of uncertainty or doubt. Rather, Camus presents us with appeals, evocations of desire, and persuasive metaphors and images. Contrasting sharply with the longing for absolutes, Camus describes his desire to return to "what I touch, what resists me" (1955, 51), to feel not the joy of unity but the boundaries and edges of the self. He longs not only to lose himself in the wind at Djemila, but to return to his body even with all of its limits and frailties. "The important thing," to continue the bodily metaphor, "as Abbé Galiani said to Mme. d'Epinay, is not to be cured, but to live with one's ailments" (Camus 1955, 38).

While Camus defines the rebel as "a man who is on the point of accepting or rejecting the sacred and determined on laying claim to a human situation in which all the answers are human — in other words, formulated in reasonable terms" (1956b, 21), what he is trying to express is a kind of outrage at the idea of impoverishing, sacrificing, or losing the self amidst the sacred. Camus argues that unbalanced efforts to find ephemeral clarity "impoverish that reality whose inhumanity constitutes man's majesty [and are] tantamount to impoverishing him himself. I understand then why the doctrines that explain everything to me also debilitate me at the same time" (1955, 55). Camus thus refuses unity *not* on rational or skeptical grounds, but on behalf of an intense and opposing desire to preserve his own integrity and experience, which would be lost in unity, and which the clarity of the absolute could only 'impoverish' and 'debilitate'.

When asked what possible grounds an absurd person could have for critiquing existential, religious, or revolutionary doctrines, Camus claims that the absurd person rejects 'leaps' because he recognizes that they substitute false and contrived categories for 'truth'. But this invocation of 'truth', like earlier invocations of reason, doubt, and uncertainty, really serves to cover over an essentially emotional appeal. When Camus detects a leap, he rejects it not exactly because it offends his logic, but because, for him, it requires "forgetting just what I do not want to forget" (1955, 46). While perhaps less philosophically rigorous, that is, at least, a more understandable stance.

It is not clear whether Camus actually believed that his arguments about the rejection of unity were logically sound or whether he dressed them up for effect. It is tempting to speculate that Camus' descriptions of these refusals may be so elusive because they had to mask a complex ambivalence that he either could not or would not fully articulate. What is clear is that Camus' efforts to frame the contrast between the desire for and the rejection of unity in philosophical language are often belied by the underlying emotional logic with which he thought we experienced and responded to those contrasts. We hear the painful tension of being neither refused nor reunited, neither fully alone nor fully with others, neither absolutely unified nor absolutely separate. And while we are told that the absurd person is opposed by a world that refuses him, we continue to see him opposed by himself, torn between contrary desires within, and engaged in a difficult resistance against himself that will form the cornerstone of absurd rebellion.

Conclusion

What is the absurd person to do when faced with this conflicted condition? If he or she refuses to yield to either desire, then what course of action remains? While the answer to these questions must form the subject of another paper, for now, I will merely reflect upon Camus' reply and suggest its relationship to the management of ambivalence discussed in the paper's first section:

> The first, and after all, the only condition of my inquiry is to preserve the very thing that crushes me, consequently to respect what I consider essential in it. I have just defined it as a confrontation and an unceasing struggle. And carrying this absurd logic to its conclusion, I must admit that that struggle implies a total absence of hope (which has nothing to do with despair), a continual rejection (which must not be confused with renunciation), and a conscious dissatisfaction (which must not be compared to immature unrest). Everything that destroys, conjures away, or exorcises these requirements (and to begin with, consent which overthrows divorce) ruins the absurd and devaluates the attitude that may then be proposed. The absurd has meaning only in so far as it is not agreed to. (1955, 31)

Here, we notice not only the precise qualification of the *emotions* of absurdity (an absence of hope that is not despair and a rejection that is not renunciation), but that the ambivalence of the absurd entails an ambivalent attitude toward absurdity, itself. The absurd must be 'preserved' even though it crushes us. It must be 'struggled against', but never 'ruined'. It must 'have meaning', but must not be 'agreed to'. Elsewhere, Camus will tell us that the absurd rebel must be "faithful to the absurd commandments" (1955, 34), while, at the same time, "the absurd requires not to be consented to" (1955, 35). Eventually, the absurd rebel must undertake the "discipline the mind imposes upon itself, that will conjured up out of nothing, that face-to-face struggle" (1955, 55), which is a struggle against himself and against the temptations of yielding to either one of his ambivalent desires. The absurd rebel's mental discipline, his struggle against himself, is analogous to the developmental ideal of mature integration of ambivalence, and that the first step of absurd morality is being able to remain in what Camus calls "extreme tension" (1955, 55), which we may imagine as a kind of 'absurd position' with respect to ambivalence.

In *The Myth of Sisyphus*, Camus' central question is whether we can survive absurdity, or if the experience is so painful that it must end in suicide. Of course, his answer is that we must never choose suicide, neither the physical nor the metaphorical 'intellectual' kind, but must seek to remain in perpetual ambivalence. Rebellion, he says, is "a matter of living and thinking with those dislocations, of knowing whether one had to accept or refuse. There can be no question of masking the evidence, of suppressing the absurd by denying one of the terms of the equation. It is essential to know whether one can live with it or whether, on the other hand, logic commands one to die of it... The danger... lies in the subtle instant that precedes the leap. Being able to remain on that dizzying crest — that is integrity" (Camus 1955, 50).

Absurd rebellion, then, is ambivalent rebellion, a complex, integrative activity that "expresses an aspiration to order" (Camus 1956b, 23), while at the same time, denying and refusing order by living "without appeal" (Camus 1955, 53). The absurd rebel "attacks a shattered world in order to demand unity from it" (1956b, 23-24), while simultaneously insisting that the world remain shattered by living "solely with what he knows" (1955, 53). Thus, rebellion is a mature and creative response to absurdity, seeking both unity and limits in an attempt to contain the destructive potential of conflicting impulses. In the absurd context, we rebel best when we recognize our ambivalence and act responsibly upon that recognition, when we neither crush it nor allow it to crush us, when as Germaine Brée put it, "our consciousness of [the absurd's] existence is followed by the refusal to be obsessed and paralyzed by it" (Brée 1964, 210-211). In this way, Camus' philosophy of the absurd addresses itself to the persistent human problems of emotional conflict, our appetite for absolutes, and the attraction of extremes, ultimately recommending a combination of maturity, reflexive awareness, and the acceptance of ambivalence to contend with them.

Bibliography

Abel, Donald. 1989. *Freud on instinct and morality*. Albany: State University of New York Press.

Alford, C. Fred. 1989. *Melanie Klein and critical social theory: An account of politics, art, and reason based on her psychoanalytic theory*. New Haven, CT: Yale University Press.

Benjamin, Lorna. 1993. *Interpersonal diagnosis and treatment of personality disorders*. New York: Guilford.

Bleuler, Eugen. 1912. *The theory of schizophrenic negativism*. Trans. W. White. Nervous and Mental Disease Monograph Series 11. New York: Journal of Nervous and Mental Disease Publishing Company. (Orig. pub. 1910.)

————. 1950. *Dementia praecox or the group of schizophrenias*. Trans. J. Zinkin. Monograph Series on Schizophrenia 1. New York: International Universities Press. (Orig. pub. 1911)

Brée, Germaine. 1964. *Camus*. Revised / First Harbinger Books ed. New Brunswick, NJ: Rutgers University Press.

Breuer, Josef and S. Freud. 1895. Studies on hysteria. In *The Standard edition of the complete psychological works of Sigmund Freud*, 2. London: Hogarth Press.

Camus, Albert. 1955. *The myth of Sisyphus and other essays*. Trans. J. O'Brien. First Vintage International ed. New York: Vintage. (Orig. pub. 1942.)

————. 1956. *The rebel: An essay on man in revolt*. Trans. A. Bower. First Vintage International ed. New York: Vintage. (Orig. pub. 1951.)

Castles, Stephen. 1998. Globalization and migration: Some pressing contradictions. *International Social Science Journal* 50 (156): 179-186.

Chan, Joseph and B. McIntyre, eds. 2001. *In search of boundaries: Communication, nation-states, and cultural identities.* Advances in Communication and Culture. Westport, CT: Ablex.

Cooper, Steven and D. Arnow. 1984. Prestage versus defensive splitting and the borderline personality: A Rorschach analysis. *Psychoanalytic Psychology* 1 (3): 235-248.

Cruickshank, John. 1960. *Albert Camus and the literature of revolt.* New York: Oxford University Press.

Freud, Sigmund. 1900. *The interpretation of dreams.* Trans. A. Brill. New York: Modern Library.

———. 1909/1955. Analysis of a phobia in a five-year-old boy. In *Two case histories: 'Little Hans and the 'Rat Man'.* Standard Edition of the Complete Psychological Works of Sigmund Freud 10, 5-149. Trans. and ed. J. Strachey. London: Hogarth.

———. 1912/1958. The dynamics of transference. In *The case of Schreber, papers on technique, and other works.* Standard Edition of the Complete Psychological Works of Sigmund Freud 12, 97-108. Trans. and ed. J. Strachey. London: Hogarth.

———. 1915/1957. Repression. In *On the history of the psychoanalytic movement, papers on metapsychology, and other works.* Standard Edition of the Complete Psychological Works of Sigmund Freud 14, 146-158. Trans. and ed. J. Strachey. London: Hogarth.

———. 1915b/1957. The unconscious. In *On the history of the psychoanalytic movement, papers on metapsychology, and other works.*

Standard Edition of the Complete Psychological Works of Sigmund Freud 14, 166-216. Trans. and ed. J. Strachey. London: Hogarth.

———. 1917/1957. Mourning and melancholia. In *On the history of the psychoanalytic movement, papers on metapsychology, and other works.* Standard Edition of the Complete Psychological Works of Sigmund Freud 14, 243-258. Trans. and ed. J. Strachey. London: Hogarth.

———. 1925/1959. Inhibitions, symptoms, and anxiety. In *An autobiographical study, inhibitions, symptoms and anxiety, the question of lay analysis, and other works.* Standard Edition of the Complete Psychological Works of Sigmund Freud 20, 87-172. Trans. and ed. J. Strachey. London: Hogarth.

———. 1959. *Group psychology and the analysis of the ego.* Trans. J. Strachey. New York: W.W. Norton. (Orig. pub. 1921.)

———. 1961. *Civilization and its discontents.* Trans. J. Strachey. New York: W.W. Norton. (Orig. pub. 1930.)

———. 1963. *Three case histories.* First Touchstone ed. New York: Touchstone. (Orig. pub. 1909-1918.)

———. 1966. *Introductory lectures on psychoanalysis.* Trans. J. Strachey. New York: W.W. Norton. (Orig. pub. 1916-1917.)

Geertz, Clifford. 1968. Ritual and social change: A Javanese example. In *Comparative perspectives on social change*, ed. S. Eisenstadt, 94-113. Boston: Little, Brown, and Company.

Gergen, Kenneth J. 2000. *The saturated self: Dilemmas of identity in contemporary life.* New York: Basic Books.

Giddens, Anthony. 1991. *Modernity and self-identity: Self and society in the late modern age.* Stanford, CA: Stanford University Press.

Giovacchini, Peter. 1982. *A clinician's guide to reading Freud.* New York: Jason Aronson.

Graubert, David and J. Miller. 1957. On ambivalence. *Psychiatric Quarterly* 31 (1): 458-464.

Greenberg, J. and S. Mitchell. 1983. *Object relations in psychoanalytic theory.* Cambridge, MA: Harvard University Press.

Harrist, Steve. 2006. A phenomenological investigation of the experience of ambivalence. *Journal of Phenomenological Psychology* 37 (1): 85-114.

Hopwood, Christopher and L. Morey. 2007. Psychological conflict in borderline personality as represented by inconsistent self-report item responding. *Journal of Social and Clinical Psychology* 26 (9): 1065-1075.

Kernberg, Otto. 1975. *Borderline conditions and pathological narcissism.* New York: Jason Aronson.

———. 1984. *Severe personality disorders: Psychotherapeutic strategies.* New Haven, CT: Yale University Press.

Kiesler, Donald. 1996. *Contemporary interpersonal theory and research.* New York: Wiley.

Klein, Melanie. 1975. *The writings of Melanie Klein, vol. 1: Love, guilt, reparation and other works, 1921-1945.* New York: Free Press.

———. 1975b. *The writings of Melanie Klein, vol. 3: Envy and gratitude and other works, 1946-1963.* New York: Delacorte / Seymour Lawrence.

Koch, Philip. 1987. Emotional ambivalence. *Philosophy and Phenomenological Research* 48 (2): 257-279.

Lifton, Robert Jay. 1993. *The protean self: Human resilience in an age of fragmentation.* Chicago: University of Chicago Press.

Lorenz-Meyer, Dagmar. 2001. The politics of ambivalence: Towards a conceptualisation of structural ambivalence in intergenerational relations. Gender Institute New Working Paper Series 2, 1-23.

Merton, Robert with E. Barber. 1976. *Sociological ambivalence and other essays.* New York: Free Press.

Minsky, Rosalind. 1998. *Psychoanalysis and culture: contemporary states of mind.* New Brunswick: Rutgers University Press.

Robertson, Roland. 1995. Globalization: Time-space and homogeneity-heterogeneity. In *Global modernities*, ed. M. Featherstone, S. Lash, and R. Robertson, 25-44. London: Sage.

Segal, Hanna. 1964. *Introduction to the work of Melanie Klein.* New York: Basic Books.

Zielyk, Ihor. 1966. On ambiguity and ambivalence. *Pacific Sociological Review* 9 (1): 57-64.

Journal of Camus Studies – Manuscript Submission Guidelines

Mission & Scope:

The *Journal of Camus Studies* is an interdisciplinary forum for scholarly conversation about the life and work of Albert Camus. The *Journal of Camus Studies* was founded in 2008 by Simon Lea as the *Journal of the Albert Camus Society*. The inaugural volume brought together the work of international authors exploring Camus's *oeuvre* from a variety of theoretical perspectives. In 2010, Peter Francev was appointed General Editor in an effort to locate the Journal at the center of contemporary academic debate and discussion about Camus. The goal of the journal is to provide a genuinely international and interdisciplinary resource for furthering the thought of Albert Camus and his contemporaries.

Manuscripts:

Abstracts:

Prior to manuscript submission, authors are asked to submit the following: full contact information along with a brief abstract of no more than 250 words.

Manuscript Preparation:

Manuscripts should be no longer than 6-7,500 words (text and notes); however, shorter papers will be considered as well. The entire paper must be double-spaced, with one-inch margins and 12-point font, in MS Word. Both the paper and notes must conform to the *MLA Style Manual and Guide to Scholarly Publishing*, 3rd edition, or *The Chicago Manual of Style*, 15th edition. They must avoid sexist and ethnic biases, be written in English. Manuscripts must not be under consideration by another publication. Along with the manuscript, the author must prepare a separate file as a cover letter. This file will include a history of the manuscript, whether it is derived from an M.A. or Ph.D. thesis with the advisor's name, whether it has been presented at a conference, or other pertinent information about its development. Authors are encouraged to submit all materials using MS Word to the General Editor who, then, will forward the materials to the review committee.

Review Process:

The *Journal of Camus Studies* follows a policy of double-blind peer review; please ensure that all author information appears only in the cover sheet document and that the main text of the manuscript contains no identifying marks. All comments by reviewers are confidential and shall not be published. Final judgment with regard to publication is made by the General Editor.

Upon receipt of submission, the Editor may conduct an initial review to determine that the manuscript is suitable for publication in the Journal. The Editor may then decline to pass the manuscript on for review or may pass the submission on to at least two editorial reviewers. At least two reviewers will provide evaluative comments and recommendations for each submission they receive. On the basis of these reviews, the manuscript may be rejected, rejected with the opportunity to revise and resubmit, conditionally accepted, or unconditionally accepted for publication. Each submitter will be provided with the peer review statements and may respond to the comments, ask questions, or seek clarification as desired. Evaluations typically require 6-8 weeks. Standard evaluation forms are used by the reviewers. The Editor and Associate Editors always seek to find the most qualified reviewers to evaluate submissions.

Deadline:

Submission deadline: 31 June of each year. This allows the reviews committee ample time to review submissions, and still permit for revisions prior to publication.

Conference Announcements and Book Reviews:

Announcements and correspondence regarding conferences, panels, papers, and other news of interest should be sent to the Editor, *Journal of Camus Studies*, at the address given below.

Books to be reviewed will be reviewed as long as they are relevant to the life and times of Albert Camus. Books should be sent to the Editor, *Journal of Camus Studies*, at the address given below.

Professor Peter Francev
Editor, *Journal of Camus Studies*

Dept. of English
Mount San Antonio College
1100 N. Grand Ave
Walnut, California 91789-1399

pfrancev@mtsac.edu
camus.society.us@gmail.com